Global Concepts for Young People

Learn how to teach global concepts and use them to increase critical thinking across the curriculum. In this new book from popular consultant Becky Hunt, you'll get ready-to-use lesson plans, stories, and activities to help you teach five key global concepts—Change, Interdependence, Culture, Scarcity, and Power. Aligned with both the C3 Social Studies Framework and the Common Core State Standards for English Language Arts, these engaging lesson plans encourage critical thinking skills that will lead to increased creativity in problem solving.

This book is an essential resource for teachers looking to:

- Create a framework to teach young people global concepts that will help them analyze and understand the world.
- Present stories and lessons connected to real-world issues that inspire students to develop innovative solutions.
- Engage students in lessons that will help them to understand and celebrate people from different cultures at home and around the world.
- Shape students into global citizens with an understanding of the world and a desire to bring about change.

Special features include anchor stories, games, graphic organizers, and critical-thinking questions. Many of the tools are available as eResources on our website, routledge.com/9781138237940, so you can print and use them in your classroom immediately.

Becky Hunt is an educator, educational consultant, and children's author who has been the principal of both public and private schools. She specializes in teacher training and staff development, curriculum studies, international studies, balanced literacy, and leadership coaching and training. Her website is www.beckyhunt.net.

Also Available from
Routledge Eye On Education
(www.routledge.com/eyeoneducation)

Global Concepts for Young People

Stories, Lessons, and Activities to Teach Children About Our World

Becky Hunt

Routledge
Taylor & Francis Group

NEW YORK AND LONDON

First published 2018
by Routledge
711 Third Avenue, New York, NY 10017

and by Routledge
2 Park Square, Milton Park, Abingdon, Oxon, OX14 4RN

Routledge is an imprint of the Taylor & Francis Group, an informa business

Library of Congress Cataloging-in-Publication Data
A catalog record for this book has been requested

ISBN: 978-1-138-23793-3 (hbk)
ISBN: 978-1-138-23794-0 (pbk)
ISBN: 978-1-315-29867-2 (ebk)

Typeset in Palatino
by Florence Production Ltd, Stoodleigh, Devon, UK

Visit the eResources: routledge.com/9781138237940

Contents

Meet the Author

Becky Hunt is an educator, educational consultant, and children's author who has been the principal of both public and private schools.

Her most recent experience is as an advisor and trainer for government schools in both Abu Dhabi and Malaysia, expanding her international perspective in education. Presently, she is working as a trainer, advisor and coach for schools in the area of literacy as an Education Support Specialist.

Becky has focused her career on helping schools to improve their strategies in teaching and creating nurturing environments where children come first. Her passion for helping teachers gain new strategies has helped to make a difference in the schools she has worked. Moreover, her global experience has broadened her insights by giving her exposure to great teachers in a variety of cultures enhancing the lives of the children they teach every day.

Her first children's book, *My Grandma's Crazy* (Ambassador International, 2014) is a tribute to today's grandmothers and a delight to both children and grandparents. Becky has visited many schools in the metro Atlanta area to share her book as a visiting author.

Areas of Specialization

- Teacher training and staff development
- Leadership coaching and training
- Balanced Literacy Program
- International Studies
- Dual Language Bilingual Program (English/Spanish)
- Educational Leadership—L-5 certification in Georgia

Becky is from Michigan and today lives in Atlanta, Georgia. Her daughter, Chelsea, and her husband, Leslie, and her two grandsons, Mason and Carter, also live in Atlanta.

If you would like Becky to provide Global Concepts training for your staff, or to learn more about Becky and contact her visit: www.beckyhunt.net.

eResources

Color versions of the concept cards in this book are available on our website as free resources. To access them, please go to the book's product page on our website, routledge.com/9781138237940. Click on the tab that says eResources and they will begin downloading to your computer.

Acknowledgments

This book wouldn't be possible if it weren't for the support of my friends and colleagues that have encouraged me throughout the process. Thank you, for your patience as you listened to stories, and gave me thoughtful feedback and new ideas. You showed me that you believed in the project and that is what motivated me to keep writing!

I want to give special thanks to John Fayad, my literary coach, for believing in me and pushing me to write the chapter abstracts and book proposal. Without your help I wouldn't have known where to start!

I would like to say thank you to my dear friend and colleague, Sue Hinton, for her thoughtful and meticulous critiquing and editing throughout the process. Your input was valuable to me and opened up my thinking to a broader, international, focus. I am proud that my book has a stamp of approval from a great Australian educator!

Thank you, to Carol Kammerman, my smart technology friend, for reading my book and providing great ideas for online resources to help teachers and students to connect to the world.

Thank you to Garden Hills Elementary School in Atlanta Public Schools and to my daughter, Chelsea Adebayo, for allowing me to pilot Global Concepts lessons in her second grade classroom, and for her patience and constant support throughout the process. You welcomed me into your classroom and we had fun co-teaching many of the lessons in my book. I loved watching you teach the lessons and model strategies that your students showed great interest in and that helped them complete the lessons and activities successfully. You are an awesome teacher and I learned a lot from you!

Finally, I want to give special mention to the many teachers that I worked with at Lincoln International Studies School, The Alfred and Adele Davis Academy, and The Maccabi Academy. Working together with you to apply the Global Concepts to your curriculum and school focus gave me a foundation to write this book. I hope that you will enjoy teaching the new lessons and stories I have written for you to share with your students!

Becky Hunt

10 Ways to Talk to Students about Sensitive Issues in the News. (NYT-The Learning Network-March 23, 2012)

1. Create a safe, respectful, and supportive tone in your class.
2. Prepare yourself.
3. Find out what students already know or have experienced.
4. Compile the students' questions and examine them together.
5. Make connections.
6. Have students investigate and learn more.
7. Explore students' opinions and promote dialogue.
8. Be responsive to feelings and values.
9. Make home connections. (Let parents know what you are talking about in class.)
10. Do something—take action. (Give students an opportunity to help.)

1

Introduction to Global Concepts

When I was a young girl, I lived on a farm and everyone at school looked like me. "Diversity" was not the catchphrase it is today. The term "Global" didn't even exist. Yet, we kept a globe in our classroom and we knew there were countries around the world where people lived differently. The *World Book Encyclopedia* and the *National Geographic Magazine* served as our main sources of information about different cultures around the world. But the people we saw in the photos lived far away and had little to do with our lives.

My small world was constant and safe. Whatever happened in distant lands remained a mystery to me and had little impact on how I lived at the time. At least that is what I thought.

Children today live in a very different world. One classroom may have students who come from all over the world. Children meet children from families that adhere to different belief systems, eat different foods, and wear different clothing. And of course there are also schools where children are isolated and do not have the opportunities to experience and learn about other cultures. So how can we help children to become Globally Aware and celebrate the beauty and richness of the cultures and people around the world?

The even bigger question is how do we help children understand the world? Events unfold around us every day. The Internet, television, and social media bring the world into our classrooms and living rooms. Turning off the TV is not always enough as news of events cause a ripple throughout the community. Children are perceptive and they become aware that a crisis has occurred somewhere in the world. Sometimes tragedy strikes in our neighborhoods, our communities, and even at home. How do we speak to children about war, poverty, and natural disasters? How do we help children understand problems and issues in the world? How do we help them to feel safe and protected? How do we give them hope?

On 9/11, I was the principal of an International Studies School in Kalamazoo, Michigan. It was a quiet morning. Students and teachers had arrived at school and were involved in their morning lessons and activities. I had completed my usual morning classroom visits and was settled into my office to tidy up unfinished paperwork when a phone call came in from a parent alerting me that a plane had flown into the Twin Towers in New York City.

I went into the library and turned on a television and was shocked at the scene unfolding before my eyes—on national TV.

The buzz went through the school from teacher to teacher and some televisions in classrooms were turned on. Students in the upper grades were watching the event with their teachers. When the reality of what was really happening hit, I went from class to class asking teachers to turn off the televisions.

The phones in the office started to ring with questions from frightened parents: "Were we aware?" "Are we going to close school?" "Are children going onto the playground?" They all expressed serious concerns of parents who were also anxious as the drama unfolded.

Never before in the history of the United States had we dealt with a terrorist attack of this magnitude on our soil. This was new territory for us at school and nothing in our handbook prepared us for handling this situation. We were soon informed by the superintendent's office that the school day would go on as normal and that teachers were not to share any information with their students about the events.

Students went through the day and played outside at recess. It felt eerie on the playground. There wasn't a plane in the sky. The world had suddenly become quiet. Children played ball, skipped rope, and slid down slides unaware that the world they lived in had changed forever.

Teachers were stunned by the events of 9/11. We met after school to share our thoughts and feelings and we agreed not to approach the subject the next day unless the students brought it up. We had no idea how much children would know, what they could absorb about the event, and if they could even begin to comprehend what had happened. Of course, we all agreed the main thing was to help our children feel safe. Reassuring them of their safety was essential to helping them not to worry that maybe this could happen at school or home.

The next day the students arrived and began to ask questions and share what they had heard as soon as they stepped off the bus. Young children understood that a tower had tipped over and a plane had crashed. Older children knew that people had died.

The teachers handled the day with the children beautifully and reassured them first that they were safe at school. The younger children seemed to quickly settle into their day and forget the incident. However, the older children worried. They wanted to talk.

Our school was an International Studies Magnet School and our curriculum centered on the five Global Concepts. These concepts were used by teachers to structure the discussions the older children were having in the classrooms.

The Five Global Concepts

1. Change—to make or become different over time.
2. Interdependence—that all things are connected.
3. Culture—the way of life of a group of people, which is learned.
4. Scarcity—balancing human needs and wants with the earth's resources.
5. Power—the ability to control something or someone else.

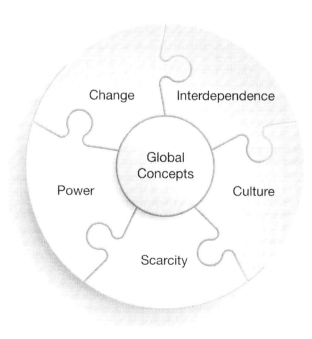

The planned lessons for the morning were put aside as the teachers listened to the children. Teachers heard the children's thoughts and questions and let the Global Concepts help them to wrap their thinking around the situation as it continued to unfold and impact the world. Some teachers mapped the children's thinking on chart paper and used these five concepts to help them to wrap their hearts and their minds around these frightening and tragic events.

As children discussed the tragedy within the framework of these concepts, their fears began to subside and the tension started to ease. Understanding the Global Concepts gave them hope as they applied them to the tragic situation. Of course the first concept, *Change*, was at the center of the discussion. The world had changed and we all knew it. Americans no longer felt safe and children sensed our fears as a result of the attack. *Interdependence* came to life when students saw the support that came from the first responders and from people all around the world. Little was known at first about who the attackers were but it was obvious they had used their *Power* to cause destruction. There were no answers to "why" but the discussions did lead students to think of how they could help. Students began to think of ways they could use their power to help people in need. Classes raised money for the Red Cross and wrote letters and drew pictures for the rescue workers. In a small way they were able to help and this gave them comfort and a feeling of control. The world for us changed on 9/11 and students today will only see it as a past event in history. But for students and teachers who were at school that day, it was a life-changing event.

Today the world is all around us, in our classrooms, on television, and in our neighborhoods. The world that once seemed to be so big has become small as we are connected through social media, Internet, and television. Students are surrounded by the events of the day no matter how we may try to shield them. World situations unfold daily in our living rooms and it is even a challenge for adults to understand exactly what is happening and why.

How can we as educators and parents help our children to understand this crazy and wonderful world in which we live today? We want our children to have empathy and we want them to "Think Globally." But how can we really teach young children to understand the world around them? Teaching children to use these five Global Concepts will give them a framework to give them insight and understanding to people and events that happen around the world. As they apply the concepts to their own lives, their school and community, and the world, they will discover that people are more alike than different and what happens in one community will eventually have an impact on the world.

Why Use Concepts?

Concepts are abstract and broad so they are easy to apply to almost any subject and topic you may be teaching. They translate easily across time and are universal. When you pose a question related to a concept there is no right or wrong answer. How someone applies a concept can vary based on their culture and experience. When concepts are applied across the curriculum and grade levels, students' understanding and ability to apply the concept will become deeper.

Young children relate to the concepts that more closely relate to themselves, their family, and their community. More mature learners are able to apply these concepts to the world outside of their own experience. The application of concepts across the curriculum provides a lens for students to examine topics at a much deeper level. Using just five Global Concepts will also give students a consistent approach to help them to improve their critical-thinking and problem-solving skills.

The Five Global Concepts

1. Change—to make or become different over time.
Change is an inevitable part of life and living. All living things go through stages of development and growth. The world and its people also experience changes that impact our daily lives. Related concepts are Cause and Effect, growing up, life cycles, weather, and seasons.

2. Interdependence—that all things are connected.
We live in a world of systems that work together. We are connected to each other, our community, and the world. Each person has a role to play in a family and in the community. Countries are linked by providing goods and services to each other. Human beings, like all systems in nature, are part of a web and depend on each other. Related concepts are family, community helpers, ecosystems, habitats, economy, and trade.

3. Culture—the way of life of a group of people, which is learned.
People create social environments and systems comprised of unique beliefs, values, traditions, language, customs, and technology as a way of meeting basic human needs. Cultures are shaped by their own physical environments and through contacts with other cultures. Related concepts include family life, art and music, holidays, festivals, shelters, clothing, and daily life.

4. Scarcity—balancing human needs and wants with the earth's resources.
Scarcity is the imbalance between wants and needs. Limited available resources cause impact on the world and systems, and on deciding how resources are to be used and distributed. Related concepts include conservation of resources, recycling, community service, caring for the environment, identifying problems, and creating solutions.

5. Power—the ability to control something or someone else.
People and nations often seek the ability to control others and to impose their values and goals on them. Related concepts include authority, collaboration, competition, justice, rights, democracy, dictatorship, war, peace, and bullying. The characteristics of a good leader and development of leadership skills are also connected to the study of Power.

I Want to Teach My Students Global Concepts. Where Do I Start?

It Starts in Your Classroom!
Creating a Global Classroom Environment immerses children in culture the moment they step inside their classroom door. When students see a multicultural focus they will start to become curious about the world. By representing the countries of students in your school, students will feel pride as they see their own culture celebrated. I will give you some ideas to help you get started.

Fabric, Fiber, Tablecloths, and Shawls
When I travel I enjoy going to fabric shops to get a yard or two of colorful material to take home. It is generally very inexpensive and it is very easy to pack. I have also used wall hangings, shawls, and tablecloths that I have purchased in markets to decorate my office and classrooms. Getting creative with textiles is a great way to create a backdrop for your Global Environment. Cover your boards and drape bookcases and center tables with colorful international fabrics. If you are a seamstress you can also make pillows for your reading corner. Fabric is long lasting and can be used year after year.

Globes, Maps, Atlases, and Flags
I often visit classrooms and notice the globe is on top of a cupboard and the maps are wound up at the top of the board. When it's time to say the pledge the flag is nowhere to be found. So proudly display your country's flag. Create

an area for students to actually touch and look at a globe. Hang a map of your country and the world on the wall and make sure it is low enough for them to see it easily. Keeping a variety of atlases out for students to read and use as resource is a great way to get students interested in geography. One word of caution! The world changes, so make sure your resources are up to date!

Multicultural Books

Look through your classroom and school library for multicultural books. Group them together in your classroom library. I have spent countless hours searching for books that you can read aloud to your students that fit with each Global Concept. These books are beautifully illustrated and spin stories in ways that children will make strong connections with the characters, and they also help children to understand the Global Concept in a personal way. Read these books to your students and make them accessible for your students to enjoy. You will also enjoy reading these stories by some of the finest American and Australian children's authors. These books are included for each Global Concept in the Bibliography at the end of the chapter.

Global Concept Center

If you have space in your classroom for a designated Global Concepts Center your students will benefit from having space to explore a variety of artifacts and activities related to each Global Concept. Students can apply their knowledge of Global Concepts through reading and writing activities during center time in your language arts block. Display each Global Concept card in the center as it is introduced. Keep the concept cards on display as students learn each new concept. Global Concept Journals can be stored at the center in baskets for students to use as they complete the writing assignments and activities that are posted each week in the center.

If you don't have enough space for a designated Global Concept Center, you can create a Global Concept Activity Box. Resources and books that are needed to complete the activities can be kept in the box and be taken to students' tables where they are working.

Artifacts and Souvenirs

Many of us have collected a variety of artifacts and souvenirs from around the world that are in boxes in our closets! Here is an opportunity for you to use these precious items as a learning tool for students in your classroom. Creating a display of dolls, carved wooden statues, money, toys, and whatever other treasures you have will make a fun, hands-on activity center in your classroom. Students will learn about culture by examining the artifacts. How to teach students about culture using artifacts will be introduced in Chapter 3. Meanwhile, display a small variety of artifacts for students to look at and enjoy as they are starting to explore and appreciate culture in your classroom!

Where can I get Global Artifacts for my classroom?

Let everyone know that you are creating a Global Classroom Environment and put out the call to your friends, family, and your students' parents. Many people have material, clothes, shawls, books, artifacts, and souvenirs that they have collected and want to get out of their closets. You will be amazed at the items that will come your way! When I was the principal at the International Studies School the local museum called and donated a truck-full of authentic artifacts from around the world that they were no longer going to use. Suddenly our whole school became a Global Environment as we placed artifacts into classrooms, display cases, and the library!

Teaching the Global Concepts

Most people agree that these concepts are important for children to learn. But, how do we teach them to young children? We don't want children to feel burdened with the world's problems. We don't want to scare children by oversharing some of the realities our world is facing today and will be facing in the future. What we want to do is give students a framework for understanding the world and also create caring people who will work together with others to solve problems in the future.

The instructional strategies listed below are an excellent way to teach children about any topic, but the main focus here will be on teaching children the Global Concepts. The strategies were chosen because they provide a balance of whole-group and small-group instruction; individual, partner, and group work; and plenty of opportunities for reading and writing. The lessons are aligned with the standards for English Language Arts (ELA) and the initial lessons are often taught during the language arts block. They have rigor and promote thinking skills. Teaching children Global Concepts is not intended to replace Social Studies lessons, however Social Studies Standards are a natural connection for many of the lessons and activities and are included to show teachers the cross-curriculum connections.

Instructional Strategies

Class Meetings

Children feel comfortable sharing when they are on the carpet or sitting in a circle with their classmates. Introducing the concepts using concept cards, shared reading selections, discussions, games, and activities calls for a more personal setting. Children learn to participate in discussions, share their thoughts and ideas, and even learn to ask additional questions as they learn about each concept. Once the lessons are introduced teachers can apply each concept across the curriculum to extend and enhance their lessons.

Charting

As each concept is introduced, children's thoughts and ideas are recorded and charted on chart paper to display in the classroom. "Charting" is a powerful instructional strategy and is a great way for teachers to record students' thoughts about each topic. The charts will also be used as a learning tool for children to refer to during discussions and while they are working on their projects.

Read Aloud Stories

Read Aloud stories are a powerful way for children to learn about each Global Concept. This is a natural way for teachers to connect their ELA lessons with the Global Concepts. Children enjoy being read to and it also helps children to improve their reading comprehension as they participate in high-level discussions, lessons, and activities that are included with the stories.

Each Global Concept has both an informational and a narrative selection for teachers to use to illustrate the concept. Discussion questions and follow-up lessons and activities will give teachers a variety of tools to introduce each Global Concept.

Read-alouds are a strong focus for a good reason. Research shows that listening comprehension precedes reading comprehension, so being read to by a more "able" or competent reader enables all children to participate in a higher-level discussion about the concept being introduced. This way, children are all on a level playing field without being inhibited and feeling excluded by their reading ability.

Written Response

Students will keep a "**Global Concepts Journal**" to record what they are learning about each Global Concept. This log will give students a place to

Image 1.1 Students enjoy writing their ideas and showing what they learned in their Global Concepts Journal.

write their thoughts and record their observations. Students will maintain their Journal throughout the year and use it as a key learning tool as they learn and apply the concepts.

Writing will give students a voice and once they begin to learn about each Global Concept they will see power in their words. Not only will children be given opportunities to write about their own experiences and opinions, but they will also be given opportunities to identify problems, conduct research, and prepare projects that will enable them to share their own unique solutions to problems in the world. Teachers will easily be able to apply their Writing Standards to lessons connected to each Global Concept. Write/Pair/Share is a strategy used in many lessons to give students an opportunity to put their thoughts into writing and share their writing with others.

Project-Based Learning

Students will learn how to work together with others as they are assigned activities and projects that are done with a partner or in a cooperative group. Learning how to work with others is an important skill that lends itself well to the focus on Global Concepts. Together children will explore topics, conduct research, and prepare projects and presentations.

Hands-On Activities

Graphic organizers help students to put their thoughts and ideas into categories that will help them to analyze what they are learning. Story Maps with a focus on the Global Concepts provide opportunities to apply the concepts to stories they have read. Students will also have opportunities to create flip-books, mini books, and posters to share what they have learned with the class.

Consistent Approach to Introduction of Concepts

Each Global Concept is presented to the class in a form of mini lessons with two Read Aloud stories and a variety of lessons and activities that teachers can choose. Each concept can be introduced in 5 lessons. Lessons are aligned with Common Core ELA Standards and can be taught during the language arts block. The lessons are taught through a variety of teaching strategies that will encourage students' critical and creative thinking, cooperative learning, and problem solving and also give them many opportunities for discussion and sharing.

Time to Teach the Global Concepts

Global Concepts lessons can be taught during Language Arts or Social Studies. Each lesson is connected to Common Core Language Arts Reading Standards and the C3 National Social Studies Standards. There are five lessons to choose from as you introduce each concept. Giving your class time for the lessons and activities is important, so don't try to squeeze lessons into your already full day. Set a consistent schedule for the Global Concepts lessons and make it part of your instructional calendar and routine.

Additional Lessons and Resources

At the end of each chapter you will find a resource section with additional lesson ideas: the "Big Ideas" about the concept, vocabulary, technology resources, and a bibliography of additional read-aloud stories that demonstrate each concept.

Suggested Timeline to Introduce the Concepts

September—Change
October—Interdependence

November–December—Culture
January—Scarcity
February—Power

This timeline is flexible and should be adapted to begin the first week of school in your district. Introducing one concept per month gives teachers and students time to do additional projects and apply the concept across the curriculum. Once students have an understanding of the concept they are ready to learn another. Once students have learned all five concepts they will be able to apply them across the curriculum and this will enhance their critical-thinking skills.

Students Learn to Apply the Concepts

Once students have been introduced to the Global Concepts they will begin to apply them in ways that we can't even imagine. When everyone is using the same language of Global Concepts you will start to see a change in how children think and react to their learning. As the school principal I can

Image 1.2 Teaching children Global Concept lessons in a cozy setting encourages students to process their own thinking and share their ideas.

remember children coming into my office to discuss issues on the playground, using the words *Power* and *Scarcity* to describe situations. "We have a scarcity of soccer balls . . ." This gave me an opportunity to give students the chance to problem-solve. "Tony is being a 'Bully' and using his power to make me mad!" Again, using the concept of Power, I could help the two students resolve their conflict. Parents also reported to me that their children used these terms at home and that they were amazed at the children's understanding and application of the concepts.

As I begin to show you how to introduce and teach each concept, keep in mind that the reason we are teaching children Global Concepts is to help them to understand the world around them, to create Global Citizens who have a heart for Social Justice, and to create Problem Solvers who will help to make our world a better place.

2

Change

It's All Around Us

> Change will not come if we wait for some other person, or if we wait for some other time. We are the ones we've been waiting for. We are the change that we seek.
>
> —Barack Obama

The first Global Concept that children need to understand is Change. The world can change in an instant or it can change slowly, but change is inevitable. Looking at the past to see how the world has changed is an important part of understanding this concept.

Learning about CHANGE

Change happens and we can do little to stop it. As adults we know this and are better prepared to handle changes when they come. But children have limited experience and understanding of changes and how to respond to change. We often celebrate changes such as birthdays, graduations, and new babies. But guess what, even those happy events bring new changes that can rock the boat a bit as we are adjusting.

Of course, there are also the tough changes that happen in our families and in the world around us. As parents and teachers, we want to shelter our children from difficult changes, but sometimes that is not possible. What we can do is help children to learn from the changes they are already experiencing. They are looking to the adults around them to model and share how we adapt to changes in a positive way. We must also give our children opportunities to talk about the changes that are happening in their lives. How we feel about change will determine how we deal with change. Learning to accept a change in a positive way is a very important life skill. Helping young children understand change is a great first step in helping them respond to change in a positive and productive way.

Changes Our Children Will Face in the World

Every generation experiences changes in the world and that is a very real part of life. My generation has seen the explosion of technology that has impacted our daily lives. We now use the Internet to find information, Google Earth to look at the world, Skype to speak face to face with people; we conduct meetings online and communication with our friends and family is virtually instant through texting on our cell phones. Every generation experiences changes and every change impacts how we live our daily lives. So how can we prepare our students for change? What changes will they be facing in their future?

One of the biggest changes that is predicted is the increase of the world population and a major shift in where people in the future will live. It is estimated by the UN that the population of the world will increase from 7.3 billion people today to 9.7 billion by the year 2050. This growth will mainly be in developing countries (United Nations Dept. of Economics and Social Affairs, June 13, 2013, New York).

So the question is how will we be able to provide housing as the population grows and becomes even more urbanized? How will we provide people with clean water and food? What impact will so many people living together on this earth have on our culture and the way we live our daily lives?

I don't have the answer, and it is likely that you don't either! These are just some of the issues that our students will face and they will be the ones who will find ways to solve each one of these problems. We can prepare our students for the future by teaching them about the concept of change and helping them to see that one change always leads to another. Understanding change and learning to adapt to change are important skills for our children to have both now and in the future. But even more important than that is the concept that people can solve problems and make changes that will help to make the world a better place.

Introducing the Global Concept—CHANGE

There are many changes for children when a new school year begins. Starting school is a common experience for children all around the world. This is the best time to introduce the concept of "Change." Making new friends, meeting new teachers, and stepping into new classroom environments are at the same time both exciting and a little scary. Lessons and activities for the Global Concept of "Change" will help students to cope with and understand change in a very personal way. It will also be a wonderful way for you, the teacher, to make connections with your students starting on the very first day of school.

LESSON 1

Introduction to Global Concepts

Key Standards

- **D2.Geo.3.K–2:** Use maps and globes to identify cultural and environmental characteristics of a place.
- **D2.Geo.4.K–2:** Explain how weather, climate, and other environmental characteristics affect people's lives in a place or region.
- **D2.Geo.4.3–5:** Explain how culture influences the way people modify and adapt to their environments.

Objectives

- I can use a globe to identify different parts of the world and explain how the environment can impact the way people live.
- I can recognize and express my feelings about changes that happen in my own life and the world.

Focus Skill: Map Identification

Activity 1: Begin Thinking Globally

Students will look at Globes and Maps of the World and brainstorm a list of questions to help them to begin thinking about the world, the people who live there, and the environment. The idea of thinking "Globally" starts with the first lesson.

Procedure

Display a Globe and give students an opportunity to identify the continents and countries they are familiar with. Point out various locations and discuss the climate based on each location's distance from the equator. What do they know about the people who live in various places around the world? Where is their family from? Following the discussion, ask students to think about questions that they have about the world using the "I Wonder" strategy.

"I Wonder" Strategy

On chart paper write, "I Wonder."

Model for students your own thinking and questioning starting with, "I wonder."

List their questions (example):

I Wonder . . .
–   How many people live in the world?
–   What is it like to live close to the equator?
–   How long does it take to fly around the world?

Tell students that this year they will explore 5 Global Concepts that will help them to get the answers to some of their questions and to understand themselves and the world around them.

Introduce the 5 Global Concepts and the Global Concepts Cards. Tell them that the first concept they will learn about is Change.

CHANGE

To make or become different over time

Compelling Question

How can lessons learned from the past help us to make positive changes in the future?

Activity 2: Introduction to Change

Ask students this question: **What is Change?** Following a discussion share the Concept Card for Change and read the definition.

Discussion and Charting Activity

Ask students to think about the changes they have already faced this year since school started. Post the questions listed below to get them started.

1. What changes have you experienced at school and at home since the first day of school?
2. How did you feel about the changes before and after they happened?

Chart student responses using the graphic organizer in Table 2.1 to record their thinking. Chart the changes in column one. In column two ask students to tell how they felt about the change. Point out to the students that all of the changes they are facing are a natural part of growing up.

Image 2.1 Charting helps students to develop a deeper understanding of each story and lesson.

Table 2.1

Changes at the start of the school year	My feelings about the change
Riding a new bus	I was scared I would miss the bus. I don't worry about missing the bus now and I like my bus driver.
Meeting new classmates	I was scared no one would like me. I made new friends and I like my class.
New Teacher	At first I was scared but I like my new teacher now and she is helping me learn.

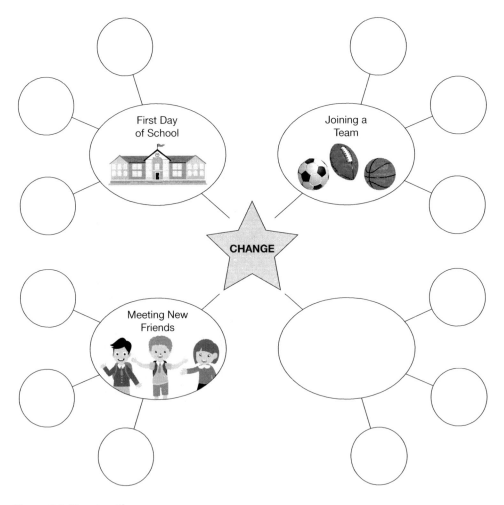

Figure 2.1 Mapping Change.

Write/Pair/Share

Students will keep a **Global Concepts Journal** to record their thoughts and what they have learned about each concept through writing assignments and activities. Give your students an opportunity to design and decorate the cover and start the first page with the definition of the Change and the compelling question.

Journal Response to Lesson 1

Grades K–2: Draw a picture and describe at least one change you have experienced since school started and show your feelings about the change.

Grades 3–5: Create a cartoon to show changes you have experienced and how you felt about them since the first day of school.

When students have completed their journal entry give them an opportunity to share their writing with a partner.

LESSON 2

Read Informational Text, "Change, It's All Around Us"

Key Standards

- **D2.His.14–K–2:** Generate possible reasons for an event or development in the past.
- **D2.His.14–3–5:** Explain possible causes and effects of events and developments in the past.
- **CCRI.3:** Describe the relationship between a series of historical events, scientific ideas, or concepts in a text using language that pertains to time, sequence, and cause/effect.

Objective

- I can determine the cause and effect of changes to help me to understand how the past impacts the future.

Focus Skill: Cause and Effect

Activity 1: Change . . . It's All Around Us

Students will read the story, "*Change . . . It's All Around Us*," to spark their thinking about Change.

Procedure

Before Reading

Introduce the story and ask students to listen for all the different changes that are discussed as you read.

During Reading

Read the story to students and give them plenty of time to think and respond to questions that are embedded throughout the text.

CHANGE . . . IT'S ALL AROUND US!

Did you know that every second, of every minute, of every hour, of every day, there are changes all around you?

Your body is changing as your cells develop. Your bones grow, and your mind and your eyes see and discover new things. There are many changes happening if you just pay attention.

Sometimes you notice changes in your body. You lose a tooth, or your pants become too short, or your shoes don't fit. These changes are a sign that you are getting bigger and growing up.

There are even changes in your brain. When you learn new things at first it can seem hard, but when you keep trying a light bulb can go off, and you think, "I get it now!"

Think about how much you have changed since you were a baby. When you were little, you couldn't walk or talk and you depended on your parents to feed you, change your diapers, give you a bath, and rock you to sleep. You didn't even know that you were changing, but you were growing up and learning new things every day.

Changes happen around you every day.

Some changes you barely notice.

Can you feel the earth moving? The world is turning slowly, and you don't even notice. Yet the dark changes to light when the sun comes up, and the light changes to dark when the sun goes down.

Sometimes we get a warning that change is coming.

In the summer when you hear thunder rumbling in the distant sky you know that a rainstorm is coming. In the winter when you hear the wind begin to howl you know it might start to snow. This is a signal or a warning that change is coming. You might grab your umbrella, bundle up in warm clothes, or run for shelter.

Sometimes change happens fast.

Falling off your bike and skinning your knee can happen quickly.

Sometimes a change is slow.

Waiting nine months for a new baby sister or brother seems like a long time to wait!

Sometimes a change can make our life easier.

We don't ride in a horse and buggy anymore since Henry Ford invented the automobile.

Sometimes a change can help the world!

Martin Luther King changed the world when he shared his dream of everyone being equal.

So can you imagine a world without change? Think about it—if there were no changes time would stand still, progress in the world would stop, and you would never grow up!

So, be thankful for every little change that happens to you and every little change that you make, because it's those changes that make you a special part of our wonderful changing world!

After Reading

Discussion Questions

1. What did you learn about change from the story?
2. What are some "Big Ideas" about Change in the story?
3. What are some other changes you can think of that were not mentioned in the story?
4. How are the effects of Change presented in the text? Can you think of more examples?
5. Can a change have more than one effect? Give an example.

Informational Story Map–CHANGE

Name_____ Date_____

What is the Main Idea of the story?	List the details below that support the Main Idea:

What did you learn about CHANGE from reading the story?

What new ideas do you have to add to the story?

Figure 2.2

Activity 2: Cause and Effect Charting Activity (Whole Group)

Procedure

Lead a discussion to show that we can look at changes as a **Cause and Effect**. The change is the Cause and what happened after the change is the Effect. Identify the Cause by starting the sentence with "Because . . . ."; point out to the students that there is the word *CAUSE* in *because*. Complete the chart with the class using changes mentioned in the story and additional changes the students mention.

Table 2.2

Cause (Change)	Effects (what happened)
Because my body is growing. . .	my pants are short and my shoes don't fit.
Because the Earth is turning. . .	the sun comes up and it's daytime. The sun goes down and it is nighttime.
Because of a storm. . .	trees fall down and the power goes out.

Activity 2: Cause and Effect Flip Book (Individual Project)

Image 2.2 Cause and effect Flipbooks illustrate students understanding of the Global Concept, Change.

K-5: Ask students to choose one change they heard in the story to create their own Cause and Effect Flip Book. (Show them an example of a Flip Book you have already made as a model.)

Table 2.3

Cause	Effect
Because I have a new baby brother . . .	No one in the house can sleep because he cries all night.

On the cover of the book draw a picture and label the *Change* or *Cause*. On the inside of the book draw pictures and label the Effects of the Change. Older students can write about the change and describe more than one effect of the change. When the Flip Books are completed give students an opportunity to share their work with a partner!

Image 2.3 Students enjoy sharing their ideas with each other.

Image 2.4 Students develop language skills when they have opportunities to talk to each other.

Image 2.5 Buddies working together make learning fun!

LESSON 3

Look at the changes in me!

Key Standards

- **History-D2.His.1.K–2:** Create a chronological sequence of multiple events.
- **D2.His.1.3–5:** Create and use a chronological sequence of related events to compare developments that happen at the same time.

Objective

- I can show changes in my life by comparing my past and present to help me predict what I will be in the future.

Focus Skill: Sequencing

Activity 1: Showing Change in Your Life

Students will create a tri-fold to show how their life has changed from the past, what their life is today, and predict what their life will be in the future.

Procedure

Tell students that today they are going to look at how they have changed since they were born. Ask them to think back to when they were a baby and compare those memories to who they are today.

With the class create a chart with the words PAST, PRESENT, FUTURE. Lead questioning and a discussion about the meaning of each time period. Ask students to tell you what words they would use to talk about the past and chart their responses next to the correct time period.

PAST—Long ago, in the past, years ago, days ago, when I was young, back in the day, yesterday

PRESENT—Today, now

FUTURE—When I grow up, tomorrow, in the future, years ahead, someday

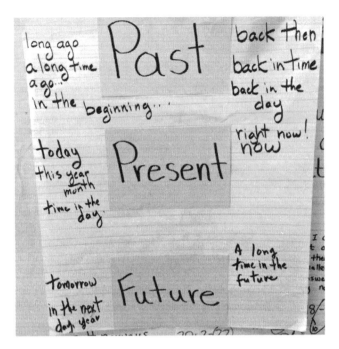

Image 2.6 Create a chart with your students to help them develop language and vocabulary that is connected to each concept.

Turn and Talk—Ask your students to think about their **PAST, PRESENT**, and **FUTURE**. Use the questions below to lead the discussion and spark their thinking! Give students an opportunity to "Turn and Talk" with their partner as you pose questions for the past, the present, and the future.

Past

When you were a baby what did you look like? Where were you born? Who took care of you? What's your birthday? Where did you live?

Present

What are you like now? What do you look like? What do you like to do? What are your favorite activities? What can you do now that you couldn't do in the past? Where do you live? Where do you go to school?

Future

What will you be like in the future? What do you think you will look like? What are your goals for the future? College? A career? Family?

Image 2.7 Flipbooks are a fun alternative to worksheets.

Activity 2: Individual Activity/Project

Students create a tri-fold and draw pictures of themselves in the past, present, and future. This will help students to see the changes that have happened in their lives and also give them an opportunity to imagine what they will be like when they are grown up.

Resources: Construction paper, crayons, and markers.

Procedure

Tell the students that they are going to create a tri-fold showing their life in the PAST/PRESENT/FUTURE. Show them an example of one that you made as a model for their own tri-fold. Students can draw pictures and label themselves at each stage or write a description below the picture.

Table 2.4

Past	Present	Future
This is me when I was a baby! I was born . . .	Here I am today. I go to Woodland School. I am in the 3rd grade. I like Baseball. I am a good reader.	This is me in the future! I am a Major League Baseball player!

Distribute construction paper, colored pencils, and crayons. Display the model and chart for students to use as they create their own tri-fold. Encourage students to include special events and information that will tell about their life during each time period.

Students complete their **Past/Present/Future** tri-folds and share with each other. Collect these to display in your Global Concepts Corner!

Read Aloud Narrative, "Changes for Charlie"

Key Standards

- **CCRL–3:** Describe characters in a story and explain how their actions contribute to the sequence of events.

Objective

- I can describe Charlie and show how he changed through the beginning, the middle, and the end of the story.

Focus Skill: Describe the main character and identify how he changes throughout the story.

Activity 1: "Changes for Charlie"

Procedure

Before Reading

Introduce the story, "Changes for Charlie." Ask students if they like change. Tell them that today they are going to hear a story about a boy who hated change. Ask them to pay attention to the changes in the story and look for changes in Charlie from the beginning to the end of the story. You can have students use the graphic organizer in Figure 2.1 as they are reading.

During Reading

As changes happen in the story pause and give students an opportunity to reflect about the change and how it is impacting Charlie. Be sure to share your thinking as a model to show students how good readers connect to the text.

CHANGES FOR CHARLIE

Charlie hated change.

He liked to wear the same clothes every day.

He wore his favorite jeans, his Superhero T-shirt, his red sneakers, and his baseball cap to school. His mother had given up getting him to wear anything else.

Charlie ate Cheerios for breakfast every morning and he always took the same lunch to school. Once again, his mother had stopped trying to get him to eat anything different.

One Saturday morning, Charlie went downstairs and his dad announced, "We're going on a little mystery trip today, Charlie. As soon as we finish breakfast, we are taking off."

"Where are we going?" Charlie asked.

"Well, that is going to be a surprise."

Charlie's heart sunk into his stomach. He was quite sure he didn't like surprises.

Mom was already packing the car and Charlie finished eating and went with his dad to get into the car. They drove for what seemed like hours before they finally turned off the highway. Charlie saw a sign that said "Welcome to River Bend."

"Well son, here we are!" said Dad.

"Is this the surprise?" asked Charlie.

"It sure is," said Mom. "This is going to be our new home! Your dad has taken a job here and we have already bought a new house. Isn't it exciting?"

Charlie looked at his mom in shock and he fought back tears. "But I don't want to move."

"I know, Charlie," she said. "It's going to be hard at first, but it's going to be a good move for our family, and you will get used to it."

The decision had been made. Charlie just sat and stared out the window as they drove past the shops and restaurants that surrounded the town square. Beyond the buildings he could see the river. It looked nice, but he was quite sure this was not a place he wanted to live.

"Change can be good, Charlie." said his dad. "You just have to give it a try. Today we will go see our new house and your new school so that you can see for yourself."

As they drove to the new house, Charlie looked out of the window and noticed a park. He cringed as he listened to his mother. "Charlie, look at that park full of kids. And a ball field! Maybe this year you can play little league! Imagine that, all this in our neighborhood. You just wait, Charlie, you are going to love it!"

Charlie just sat in the back seat and crossed his arms. He didn't like it and that was all there was to it. He liked his old house. He didn't need a new house. He hated baseball and he would never want to play in that stupid park. The car started to slow down, and they turned into the driveway of a blue house with a porch that wrapped all around the front.

They walked up the front steps and out of the corner of his eye Charlie noticed a girl watching them from next door. She waved at him, and he quickly turned around and went into the house. *A girl next door, great. This move is going to be worse than I imagined*, thought Charlie. The ride back home was quiet, and Charlie was sure that this move was a big mistake.

The next week was a blur as Charlie went to school each day and came home to discover more and more boxes piled up to get ready for the big move. His teacher had a going-away party for him, and his friends gave him gifts and cards. Charlie had so much fun that he almost forgot that the next day he was moving away.

The huge moving van showed up early, and the movers started before Charlie was even out of bed. He looked out the window and saw them carrying out the sofa, the kitchen table, chairs, and boxes. It was all going on the truck in a hurry. He reluctantly got out of bed and pulled on his jeans and his Superhero T-shirt.

Once the van was packed, they got into the car and followed the moving van to the new house. Charlie watched out the window as everything that was familiar to him disappeared and the new scenery rolled out before him.

They pulled up to the front of the house and parked as the moving van backed into the driveway. The ramp came down, and Charlie stood on the porch and watched as the furniture and boxes were moved into the new house. Mom and Dad were busy inside, telling the movers where it all went, and weren't really paying much attention to Charlie.

The next thing Charlie saw was that same girl walking toward his house and carrying a plate. *Oh, no, not her!* Charlie was thinking. He couldn't ignore her because before he knew it, she was right in front of him with a plate of delicious-smelling chocolate chip cookies.

"Hi there, I'm Marcy! My mother baked these cookies for you and asked me to bring them over. What's your name?"

"Charlie," he answered and took the plate out of her hands. "Thank you."

"Well, let's eat some!" she said, and she plunked herself down on the porch railing and grabbed a cookie. "They're still warm," she said. "Eat one, they're yummy!"

Charlie took a cookie, and he had to admit they were pretty good. Marcy started chatting and told him all about the school and the neighborhood. "I like to ride bikes, do you?" she asked as the movers took Charlie's bike off the truck. Marcy spotted it right away. "Hey, let's go on a bike ride!" Charlie did think it would be fun and ran into the house to get permission from his mom. Out he came, and he jumped on his bike and rode across the lawn to Marcy's house.

Marcy and Charlie rode their bikes through the neighborhood and to the park. Marcy introduced him to some boys who asked Charlie to play ball with them. He had fun, and by the time they got back home the moving truck was gone.

Charlie waved goodbye to Marcy and rode his bike into his driveway. He jumped off and ran up the front steps and into the house. He found his parents in the kitchen unpacking boxes. "Go up to your room and check it out. I think you will be happy," said his mom.

When he walked into his room his bed was made and he spotted his favorite pillows and stuffed animals. His T-shirt was dirty so he grabbed a blue T-shirt out of his drawer. *Maybe moving won't be so bad after all,* he thought as he pulled his clean shirt over his head and headed downstairs.

After Reading

Discussion Questions

1. How does the author show you that Charlie hated change?
2. Why do you think Charlie hated change? How do you know?
3. What happened in the story that helped Charlie feel better about the changes?
4. How did Charlie change throughout the story?
5. What did you learn about change from reading the story?

Activity 2: Whole Group Story Mapping

KG–5: Review the story with the students by charting a story map with a focus on CHANGE.

Activity 3: Independent Journal Writing

Grade KG–5: Ask students to write and/or draw pictures in their Global Concept Journals to show how Charlie changed from the beginning to the end of the story.

Table 2.5

At the beginning of the story Charlie . . .	In the middle of the story Charlie . . .	At the end of the story Charlie . . .

Story Map–*Changes for Charlie*
Name_____ Date_____

Describe Charlie	What is the main problem in the story?

List each Change Charlie went through in the story.	Tell how Charlie Felt about each change.

How did Charlie's feelings change by the end of the story?

What did you learn about, CHANGE, from reading the story?

Figure 2.3

LESSON 5

Changes in Technology

Key Standard

- **D2.His.2.K–2:** Compare life in the past to life today.

Objective

- I can compare the changes in (Toys or Technology) from the past to the present and so I can design how it might change in the future.

Focus Skill: Identify changes and improvements in technology

Activity 1: Whole Group

Students will observe a variety of toys from the past and compare them to what they are like today. They will also examine the toys to determine what the advantages and disadvantages are to each one.

Procedure

KG–2: Display or show photos of old toys and toys children play with today. Choose toys that are similar to show how they have changed and developed over time. One example is a play radio that you wind up and it plays one song. Compare that to a toy from today that plays many songs, teaches the alphabet, and needs batteries. Chart with the students the advantages and disadvantages to each toy. In the final category let them imagine what that toy might be like in the future!

Image 2.8 Toy airplane from the past.

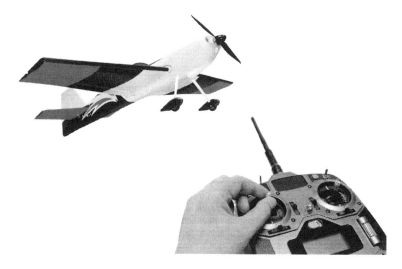

Image 2.9 Toy airplane today.

Table 2.6

	Advantages	Disadvantages
Toy from long ago		
Toy we play with today		
Toy in the future		

3–5: Display or show photos of an old corded rotary phone and a cell phone that we use today. Lead a discussion and create a chart with students to describe the changes and improvements to the phones as they evolved. What are the advantages and disadvantages of each phone? How did the change impact how people live? What changes can they imagine there will be in technology that will change phones in the future?

Image 2.10 Phone from the past.

Image 2.11 Phone from the present.

Table 2.7

	Advantages	Disadvantages
Phone from long ago		
Phone we use today		
Phone in the future		

Extension Activity—KG–2

KG–2: How people lived in the past and how they live today are very different. Students will look at how life has changed and create a foldable to compare life in the past to life today.

Procedure

Share with the students pictures of how people lived in the past. These pictures could be from the time period in history you are presently studying in Social Studies. You can show pictures from books or video clips. Lead a discussion with students about how their lives today are alike and different. Give students a plain sheet of paper to fold and label, "Life in the Past," and "Life in the present." Ask students to draw pictures and label or describe specific things that have changed from past to present.

Image 2.12 Family travel in the past.

Image 2.13 Family travel today.

Table 2.8

How people lived in the past	How people live today
It took a long time to get places in a covered wagon. They had to bring their own food and beds in the wagons. It was a difficult journey.	People can fly in a jet across the country or anywhere in the world in less than a day.

Extension Activity KG–3–5: Inventions in the Past/Present/Future

Working together with a partner or a small group, ask students to choose one invention to research. Ask them to create a presentation to show how the invention has developed and changed over time and what they predict it will look like in the future.

Give them these questions as a guideline:

1. Describe the invention and show how it changed over time.
2. How did the changes impact how people live their daily lives?
3. What are the advantages and disadvantages?
4. How has this invention changed the world?
5. Predict how the invention will change in the future.

Give students ample time to complete their research and prepare their presentations. Students will share their projects with the class and display them in the classroom.

Unit Closing Activity

Write/Pair/Share—Journal Response to Compelling Question

KG–2: With teacher support write a story and draw a picture to respond to the Compelling Question.

3–5: Write a response to the Compelling Question.

How can lessons from the past help us to make positive changes in the future?

KG–2: The graphic organizer in Table 2.9 below will help them to think of a personal example.

3–5: Students can choose a personal or historical example.

Table 2.9

Event from the past	Lessons learned	Positive changes for the future.
I received a bad report card and my parents were upset.	I felt bad because my parents were upset and I know I need to do better next time. I need to study and work harder to get good grades.	I started to write down my assignments and do my homework. I paid better attention in class. My grades improved and my parents were happy!

Give students time to organize their thoughts and write their responses. When students have completed their writing give them time to share it with a partner.

Additional Lesson Ideas and Resources

Timeline of My Life So Far: Students can create a timeline of their life starting from the day they were born. Parents can help them with dates and special events to include on their timeline. Students will see the changes they have already experienced in their lives and have fun sharing their timeline with the class!

Cause and Effect Chain Reaction: One change always leads to another! Students choose one change and then draw arrows to show the many changes that will happen as a result of the first change that happened. The chain of events organizer will help students to expand their critical thinking.

K–2 Example: Students can draw pictures to illustrate the changes that happen!

Table 2.10

Mom and dad finally let me get a new puppy.
We buy the puppy his food and a leash and a collar.
Now I have to feed the dog and walk him.
My puppy cries at night and keeps us awake.
I play with my puppy after school.
I have to clean up his messes. I still love my puppy and he gets to sleep with me!

3–5 Example:

Table 2.11

It rains for days.
The river in our town fills up
The water pours over the banks of the river and floods the land.
Water flows into the streets and houses. People get trapped and have to leave.
The rescuers come in boats to save them.
People live in a shelter until the water is gone and it is safe to return home.

Home-School Connection: Ask students to interview a parent or grandparent about the changes in technology during their lifetime. Encourage students to share what they learned with the class. You may even want to invite a guest in to share their thoughts about the changes they have seen in their lifetime!

Antique Artifact Collection: Bring in antique tools or household items to share with your class. Ask students to guess what they are and what they were used for. How does an antique item compare to the same item we use today? How did it change? Leave a variety of artifacts on the table and give students an opportunity to do their own prediction and research about the items.

Act It Out: Students work together in groups to create and present a skit about "Change." Brainstorm with the class a list of potential topics: *new teacher, new student, wearing glasses, riding the school bus for the first time, a new baby in the house, etc.* Skits should demonstrate the concept of Change and show the main character's feelings about the changes he/she faced.

News Broadcast: Students can work individually or in groups to research an event in history that created a major change in the world. Students will create a news broadcast to teach the class about the event and the impact it has made on the world!

Collage: Create a "Change" collage. Look through magazines and newspapers to find pictures that show changes. Add pictures to the collage to create a class "Change" collage.

Cartoon Strip: Create a cartoon strip about a character from a story that goes through many changes. Show the events in the story in 8 boxes showing the changes that character goes through from beginning to end. Use conversation bubbles to show their thinking and dialogue.

Creative Writing: Write a narrative story about Change. The story can be fictional or based on a personal experience.

Big Ideas about Change

- Change is a universal characteristic of all human societies.
- Communities change over time.
- There are cycles in nature and life.
- Technological advances have a major influence on change.
- People change their environment to satisfy their needs and wants.
- Changes in culture have led to conflicts within and between societies.
- Changes in human society have been gradual through evolution or sudden effects through revolution.

- Knowledge of the past is necessary to understand present and future events.
- Change produces both short-term and long-term effects.
- The economies and governments of the world are constantly changing.

Change Vocabulary

Table 2.12

Past/Present Future	Timeline	Grow	Adapt
Develop	Human Impact	Yesterday Today Tomorrow	Before During After
Compare-Contrast	Cause/Effect	Alter	History
Cycles	Evolve	Reform	Transform

Applying the Concept of Change Across the Curriculum

Social Studies: history, historical events, world events—past/present/future, famous leaders of change.

Science: life cycles, chemical changes, changes in the earth, seasons, changes in the environment, weather changes, natural disasters.

Math: changes in numbers—place value, adding/subtracting/multiplication/division, increasing and decreasing, greater than, lesser than, equal to, changing fractions to decimals/percent.

Global Concepts Read Aloud Lesson Plan

Story Title_____

Author:_____

Global Concept_____

How is the concept demonstrated?	Common Core/ELA Standard

Vocabulary	Resources: Technology Links:

Questions:

 Before-

During-

After-

Follow Up: Discussion____ Charting ___ Graphic Organizer ___ Journal Entry

Cross Curriculum Link:

Activity:

Figure 2.4

Use this graphic organizer to plan a read-aloud for the books in the bibliography or for any of the texts recommended in this book.

Global Concepts Informational Text Map

Title: Author:	Global Concept/Topic
What is the Main Idea or Theme of the text?	**List supporting details:**

What did you learn about _____ from reading the text?

What new ideas can you add?

Figure 2.5

Use the Global Concepts Informational Text Map to help students to analyze any of the nonfiction or fiction texts related to global concepts.

Narrative Story Map

Name_____

Title: Author:	Main Character (s)
Main Events in the story:	Problem/Solution:

What Global Concept was demonstrated in the story?

What did you learn about the Global Concept _____ from the story?

Figure 2.6

Use the Narrative Story Map to help students to analyze any narrative texts related to global concepts.

Bibliography for Global Concepts Books: CHANGE

Giant Steps to Change the World (K–5)

Authors: Spike and Tonya Lewis Lee
Illustrator: Sean Qualls

This motivational picture book will inspire your students to take big steps to set things right in the world. This Read Aloud is a great history lesson as children learn about people throughout history who have taken "giant steps" to change the world. Leave it to Spike Lee and his wife Tonya to create a story that illustrates the big steps we all have to make to create a positive change despite of the challenges we may face. Use this book as a kickoff to your students writing about the Giant Steps they want to take to change the world!

Our Children Can Soar: A Celebration of Rosa, Barack, and the Pioneers of Change (K–5)

Author: Michelle Cook

This book showcases African Americans who used their talents to make great changes in the world. Beautifully illustrated, it shows the courage and power that each person used to make a difference in the world. It is a simply written book that will be easy for young children to understand and get their first glimpse of some of these pioneers of change. There is a short biography about each person at the end of the book to share with the students.

Window (K–5)

Author/Illustrator: Jeannie Baker

Share this wordless picture book with your students and explore the concept of change as a mother and baby look through a window at a view of wilderness and sky as far as they can see. As Sam, the baby, grows, the view changes. This story gives a beautiful vision of the changes we see in the world while we are also growing and changing.

Pecan Pie Baby (K–2)

Author: Jacqueline Woodson
Illustrator: Sophie Blackall

One of the biggest changes a child can face is having a new baby in the house! Jacqueline tells the story of "Gia," an only child who is having a difficult time getting excited about the new baby that is coming. In fact she often refers to the new little bundle of joy as the "Ding Dang Baby!" Have fun reading this story to your class and hearing their own stories of new babies at their houses. Some of your students will be able to relate to Gia's feelings about the big change that is coming to their own lives!

Grandfather's Journey (3–5)

Author/Illustrator: Allen Say

The author, Allen Say, shares the personal story of his grandfather's journey as a young man from Japan to America. His strong desire to be in both places at once shows the feelings that I am sure immigrants who have left their homeland feel today. This heartwarming story shows the realities of the changes grandfather goes through in his lifetime.

Dandelions (2–5)

Author: Eve Bunting
Illustrator: Greg Shed

Most of us cannot imagine what it would be like to move across the country in a covered wagon, but Eve Bunting gives us a realistic picture of the hardships pioneer families faced as they settled the west in American history. The trip is unbearable to Zoe until she finds a patch of Dandelions that remind her of home and give her hope for the future.

The Keeping Quilt (2–5)

Author: Patricia Polacco

This true story illustrates the Global Concept of Change as Patricia Polacco tells us about the homemade quilt that passed through the lives of four generations of her immigrant Jewish family. As you read this story to your class use it as an opportunity to learn about quilting and quilts that share the stories of other families. Bringing in a quilt of your own or from someone in the community will be a wonderful way to show the concept of CHANGE through the beautiful patterns within the quilt.

Show Way (K–3)

Author: Jacqueline Woodson
Illustrator: Hudson Talbott
G.P. Putnam's Sons

This beautifully written and illustrated book carries on with the theme of "quilting" as a young girl learns to quilt from 'Big Mama' on the plantation. The colorful stars and moons and roads that were woven into the quilt showed the way to freedom. Quilting was passed on from generation to generation as a symbol of their culture and the struggles faced by African Americans. This story illustrates the Global Concept of Change as it shows how the lives of African Americans changed throughout American history.

Teacup (K–2)

Author: Rebecca Young
Illustrator: Matt Ottley

A young boy has to leave home and find another. In his bag he carries a book, a bottle, and a blanket. In his teacup he holds some earth from where he used to play. This is one boy's story of leaving his homeland, surviving a long journey by sea and finding a safe, new place to call home. This gorgeous book shows the changes he faces each day through its beautiful illustrations and simple words.

The Color of Home (2–5)

Author: Mary Hoffman
Illustrator: Karin Littlewood

A new student joins the class from Somalia and the children try to be friendly, but Hassan is not happy. He misses his home. He can't remember even a few English words. It's not until a very special teacher spends time with him and gives him a paintbrush that he can express his real feelings. This story is a good one to read to all students to give them an idea of what the reality of being a refugee really means.

When Jessie Came Across the Sea (3–5)

Author: Amy Hest
Illustrator: P.J. Lynch

Jessie is a young Jewish girl who moves to America from a poor village in Poland. The story of her journey and the challenges she faces show her courage as she embraces the changes she goes through and builds a new life in a city that is not her own. This story not only shows the story of Jessie, but gives us a glimpse into the lives of American immigrants that came to our country and worked hard to achieve their hopes and their dreams.

So Far From the Sea (3–5)

Author: Eve Bunting
Illustrator: Chris K. Soentpiet

Eve Bunting shares a dark period in American history in a real and thoughtful way as she tells the story of a Japanese family that visits the site where their grandfather died and their father once lived: the Manzanar War Relocation Camp site in California. The Global Concept of Change is illustrated when Japanese Americans are relocated to camps after the bombing of Pearl Harbor. The heartbreaking story and the father's ability to move forward despite the injustice that he and his family face show the amazing resilience of people when they face difficult times.

When I was Young In The Mountains (K–3)

Author: Cynthia Rylant
Illustrator: Diane Goode

What grandparent doesn't enjoy telling their grandchildren about their lives when they were young? This story does just that as grandmother shares her story growing up in the mountains with her grandparents in a coal-mining town. Read this story to your children to help them see what life was in the past and compare it to their lives today! Some things never change, and that is the love of our grandparents.

3

Interdependence

How We All Live and Work Together

> When I was a boy and I would see scary things in the news, my mother would say to me, "Look for the helpers. You will always find people who are helping."
>
> —Fred Rogers

In Chapter 3, students learn how the world and people all work together. This concept begins with a focus on the world that children understand best: their family, school, and their community. Once students see all of the people around them that help to support them every day they feel safe and loved. In turn, they begin to learn their place in the world and the important roles that they play.

Learning about Interdependence

Imagine what life would be like if we were isolated and lived totally alone? It is almost impossible for us to imagine it because we know how much we depend on each other. Yet, children think in a way that is much more self-centered. They don't realize how much they depend on others to help them to have all of their needs met, get their education, and to be safe. When we explore the Global Concept of Interdependence, children will also learn that they have a special role to play.

Teaching children Interdependence starts at the beginning of the school year when you begin building a community within your classrooms. Students are making new friends, learning to work together in groups, and the teacher is putting important routines and procedures in place that will help to create a positive learning environment. Introducing the concept of Interdependence as children are learning these new routines will help them to see how important it is for everyone to work together, follow the routines and procedures, and help each other.

Children will feel more secure once they become aware of all the people there are that give them help, guidance, and support. Encouraging children to recognize this support as part of our Interdependent world will help them to become responsible and supportive in the various roles they play as a child. Children don't often think of themselves as part of this important web of Interdependence. They will see that they are important as they follow rules, do their best work at school and at home, help people in need, and love their family and friends. In our Interconnected world everyone has an important role to play!

Connecting Interdependence across the Curriculum

The study of Interdependence also lends itself nicely to many topics across the curriculum. In Science we learn about ecosystems and habitats that are carefully balanced to support life. In Social Studies we learn about the community and community helpers who have special jobs to provide important services we need and keep us safe. Economics lessons become real as students discover how we are all connected by the transfer of goods around the world. Learning to understand the concept of Interdependence will help students to see how we all have a role to play as we live and work together at home, at school, and in our Global Community.

Interdependence Gives Children Hope

The concept of **Interdependence** is closely linked to all of the other Global Concepts and provides us with support and hope for the future. When we go through **Changes** in our lives it is the people around us who provide us with love and support, especially in tough times. Every **Culture** has a tight connection within families and communities. We look at those who are closest to us to share the good times and the bad. Whenever **Scarcity** becomes an issue, whether it be an individual, community, or an entire nation, there are people and organizations that give assistance to those in need. The final concept, **Power,** is strengthened by people who are united and work together to support individual leaders or governments in power. In turn, Power can be diminished by groups of people who stand together to fight against someone who uses their power in a negative way. It is the Interdependence of our family, our community, our nation, and the world that helps us all to live happy and productive lives.

But perhaps the most important thing that we want children to learn from the lessons we teach them about Interdependence is that they are connected and that they have their own very special role to play in this Interconnected world. Children want to be connected. When children understand that they are an important part of this Interconnected world they feel safe and secure. Knowing that there will always be someone there to give them love and support provides a sense of security that children need to grow and thrive. Teaching children the Global Concept of Interdependence is the key to giving children Hope.

Introducing the Global Concept—Interdependence

Creating a Classroom Community

Even though the first concept you teach is Change, you are already modeling the concept of Interdependence by creating a classroom community. Creating your classroom community starts on the first day of school. When your students feel connected and have a sense of belonging in their classroom you have provided one of the best examples of Interdependence for children to experience firsthand. Giving your students the feeling that they are a valued member of your class and showing them that they each have a special role to play is key to creating that classroom community feeling.

Class Meetings

Class Meetings are a perfect way for you to build trust with your students and give them a sense of community. During class meetings you can engage students in team building activities, discussions, and sharing, and of course this is a great opportunity to review important routines and procedures and the schedule for the day. Class meetings can be long or short, but the key is to have one every morning to provide a consistent and positive start to each day. In addition, a class meeting at the end of the day can provide closure and give students a time to reflect about what they learned and send them home with a positive feeling about the day and preparation for the day ahead.

As an instructional coach I visit classrooms around the world and teachers tell me they don't have time to start the day with a class meeting. The bell rings and students come into the classroom and they are expected to immediately sit in their seats and start their lessons. I know that teachers today feel pressured by the curriculum and standards they are expected to teach, but my question to them is this: How can children learn in an environment where the focus is only on the lessons of learning and not the lessons of life?

Your Global Classroom environment isn't just the displays on the walls, it is also the environment you create as you are building a community with your students. So start each day by greeting your students and making connections with each one of them through a class meeting every morning before you begin your busy day. I promise you that your students will learn better in an Interdependent classroom where every child feels connected.

LESSON 1

Introduction to Interdependence

Key Standards

- **D2.Civ.2.K–2:** Explain how all people, not just leaders, play an important role in a community.

Objective

- I can demonstrate my understanding of the Global Concept "Interdependence" to show how people are all connected.

Focus Skill: Role Playing/Teamwork

Activity 1: Creating a Web of Community

Students work together to create a web of community helpers to illustrate how people in their community are connected to support and help each other.

Resources: Chart paper, markers, string

Procedure

Pose the compelling question and facilitate a discussion with students as they share their thinking. Introduce the term Interdependence and display the Concept Card.

Table 3.1

School Helpers	Community Helpers	Family Helpers
Teacher	Policeman	Mother
Teacher Assistant	Policewoman	Father
Principal	Fireman	Sister
Assistant Principal	Mayor	Brother
Cafeteria Worker	Judge	Grandmother
Technology Specialist	Road Construction Worker	Grandfather
Parent Volunteers	Building Construction Worker	Aunt
Librarian	Postal Worker	Uncle
Office Staff	Store Clerks	Cousin
Student	Bank Teller	Friend
Bus Driver		

Brainstorm a list of School Helpers, Community Helpers, and Family Helpers

Chart students' ideas to use as a model for a Role Play activity. Here is a list of community helpers to use as a reference:

Activity 2: The Web Game

Resources: Paper plates, string, yarn, crayons, and markers

Procedure

1. Give each student a paper plate to make a sign with the name of one of the helpers from the list and a picture showing what their important job is to help the community. (For young children and ESL students, pictures of community helpers with their role and title will help their understanding.)
2. Punch a hole on the top and loop a piece of yarn and tie it so students can hang it around their necks.
3. When all students have completed their Role Plate ask them to stand up and form a circle. Ask each student to tell who they are and what they do to help the community.

Image 3.1 Playing the string game is fun and shows how we are all connected!

INTERDEPENDENCE

All Things Are Connected

Compelling Question

How are we connected to people in our family, our community, and the world?

4. The teacher starts the game by holding onto one end of the string and tossing the ball of yarn to a student. "Thank you, nurse, for helping me when I am sick."

5. That student catches the ball and says, "You are welcome!" Then he or she tosses the ball to another community helper and says, "Thank you, policeman, for making me safe." Each time a child catches a ball and throws it they hold onto the yarn. At the end of the game they will see how they are all connected.

6. Demonstrate that the web is tight and strong when they are all holding onto their piece of the web. Ask students to tell how this shows an example of Interdependence.

7. Pose this question to the class: *What will happen to the web if one by one people stop doing their jobs?* Demonstrate by asking students one at a time to let go of their part of the web and sit down. One by one the students will see that the web collapses.

8. When everyone is seated ask students to share how they felt once they saw the web starting to collapse. Remind students that everyone is responsible to each other and we all have a special role to play in our Interdependent community!

Closing Activity: Journal Reflection

Students will start a new section in their Global Concepts Journal, labeled "Interdependence."

Copy the definition of Interdependence in your Journal and the compelling question: **How are we connected to our family, our community, and the world?** Write a response to the compelling question.

K–2: Draw and label a picture to show people you are connected to your family, your community, and the world.

3–5: Describe how you are connected to people in your family, your community, and the world and explain what special roles they play.

Give students ample time to write their responses to the compelling question and share their response with a partner.

Shared Reading—Informational Text, "Interdependence . . . All Things Are Connected"

Key Standards

- **CCRI.2:** Determine main ideas of a text and explain how they are supported by key details, summarizing the text.

Objective

- I can show my understanding of Interdependence by determining the main idea and writing a summary of the key details in the text.

Focus Skill: Main Idea with details

Procedure

Before Reading

Tell your students that you are going to read them a story that will help them to understand even more about Interdependence. Ask the children to try to imagine what it would be like to be all alone as you begin to read.

During Reading

As you read the story, share your thoughts with students as you reflect upon what the text is saying. In turn ask students to share their thoughts with you.

INTERDEPENDENCE . . . ALL THINGS ARE CONNECTED

Imagine yourself all alone on this planet . . .

What would it be like if you didn't have your family, your friends, your teachers, or your neighbors? Who would you talk to? Who would you play with? How would you live on your own? The world would be a very scary place and life would be very difficult if you were all alone!

Here is the good news! You are not alone. Your family loves and cares for you. You have fun with your friends. You learn from your teachers. You depend on all of these people, and they depend on you. This is called Interdependence . . . we are all connected!

Think about this . . . when you drink a glass of milk do you ever think of how many people it took to get the milk into your refrigerator?

One morning, very, very early a farmer got up out of his bed, got dressed, and went out to his barn to milk his cows. The cows were very glad to see him because he also gives them their feed!

The milkman visited the farm to collect the fresh milk and he delivered it in his truck to the dairy. The milk was then pasteurized and bottled by the workers at the dairy.

The milk bottles were loaded into a milk truck and a truck driver took the milk to the grocery store. Then he took the milk into the store and the stock worker put the milk into the cooler.

Your mother went into the grocery store and bought the milk from the cashier who also put the milk into a bag with the other groceries. The friendly grocery bagger loaded the grocery cart and brought it to your mother's car. Mother drove home and the family helped to unload the groceries and put the milk into the refrigerator.

Whew, you can finally have a glass of milk! We depend on people just like this to help us every day and we don't even know they exist . . . this is what Interdependence is like. We all play a special role in this world and this is how we all live together.

Even in nature all things are connected. Bees and flowers depend on each other to live. The bees carry pollen from one flower to another so the flower can reproduce. In turn flowers provide food for the bees so that they can produce honey. Of course we like to eat the honey! The cycle of life is like that and the plants and animals and people all depend on each other to live.

Do you know anyone in China? You may not, but guess what . . . you depend on people in China to make many of the items you use in your home and the toys you like to play with.

Do you like to eat rice? Indonesia is one of the largest rice producers in the world. Did you ever think of how far the rice traveled before it got to your house?

Does your car need fuel? Saudi Arabia is one of the largest producers of oil in the world. We depend on them and many other countries to provide enough gasoline and oil for our cars.

And guess what, countries that you depend on also depend on other countries from around the world to supply important resources, products, and services they need to live. We are all connected and we depend on each other in our Interdependent world.

Being connected helps all of us to live full and productive lives. One person depends on countless people at home, at school, and from all around the world to make our life complete.

So what is your part to play in this Interdependent world? You may think, *I am just a child, what can I do to help?*

Believe it or not, you have a very important role to play . . .

Your family depends on you in many ways. You depend on your family to provide you with a home, a cozy bed, a yummy dinner, and lots of love. Your family depends on you to bring them joy and love. You also have a role to be responsible by helping at home and doing your best at school. You depend on your family and your family depends on you. Everyone has an important role to play.

Do you know what important roles you play at school? Your teachers get up very early in the morning, go to the school, and prepare lessons for the day. It is your job as a student to get up early, get dressed, eat a good breakfast, and get to school on time. Being a good student, participating in class, and doing your homework are also important roles that you play. When everyone does their job at school the teachers are happy and the students are learning. We are all connected at school.

But what about your important role in the world? Did you know that the world is depending on YOU? It is children, just like you, who will take care of our world in the future. Getting a good education, learning to be a caring and loving person, and working hard and being a responsible student are the most important roles children play in the world today.

So don't forget that you are not alone and people all around the world are not alone, either. When we all work together the world is a better place. Everybody has an important role to play in our wonderful, Interdependent world!

After Reading

Discussion Questions

1. What are some key points the author made about Interdependence that were new to you?
2. What examples of Interdependence were included in the text? Can you think of additional examples of Interdependence?
3. What are some roles people play in our Interdependent world? What roles do you play?
4. How are you connected to people around the world? Determine the Main Ideas about Interdependence from the text. How do you know?

Charting Activity

Together with the students determine the main idea and list the details in the story that support it.

Write/Pair/Share

KG–5: What roles do you play? Write a description and draw a picture to describe the roles that you play and the responsibilities you have in that role (daughter, son, sister, brother, student, and so forth).

Give students time to complete their Journal response and share it with a partner.

––––––––––––––––––––

Informational Story Map–INTERDEPENDENCE

Name_____ Date_____

What is the Main Idea of the story?	List the details below that support the Main Idea:

What did you learn about INTERDEPENDENCE from reading the story?

What new ideas do you have to add to the story?

Figure 3.1

LESSON 3

Shared Reading—Narrative, "The Lazy Village"

Key Standard

- **CCRL.2:** Recount stories, including fables, folktales, and myths from diverse cultures; determine the central message, lesson, or moral, and explain how it is conveyed through key details in the text.

Objective

- I can summarize the events in "The Lazy Village," and determine lessons we can learn from the story.

Focus Skill: Summarizing

Procedure

Before Reading

Ask students if they have ever noticed that some towns and neighborhoods are well taken care of and some look run down. Tell students that today's story is about a village that becomes run down and the people who live there learn a very important lesson about Interdependence!

During Reading

As you read the story pause to reflect and give students an opportunity to predict what will happen next.

THE LAZY VILLAGE

Once upon a time there was a little village nestled between two tall mountains. The village was known as the prettiest village in the land and visitors from all around came just to see it.

The houses in the village were brightly painted with gardens that were carefully groomed. The flowerpots along the streets were overflowing with petunias, daisies, and bright red geraniums. The stream that wound its way through the town was clean and pure.

The people in the village worked hard and took great pride in their homes and their families.

The shopkeepers swept the walks in front of their stores and took good care of their customers.

The mailman delivered the letters and packages house to house in a timely manner.

Teachers arrived at school early to prepare their lessons. The schoolchildren studied hard and always completed their homework.

Everybody in the village lived and worked together like one big family. Life was perfect in the village and everyone was happy. But little by little the village started to change.

It started with Mr. Parker. One day, Mr. Parker noticed the paint was peeling on his house and it needed to be painted. But he decided to wait and paint his house next year so he sat on his porch swing day after day snoozing in the afternoon sun.

Miss Bridget owned the dress shop and she was known for having the most stylish clothes in town. But one morning she slept through her alarm and didn't get up to go open the shop. Her customers banged on the door and looked in the windows, but Miss Bridget was nowhere to be found.

Mr. Bailey, the mailman, was always the first one up and he opened the post office early every morning. But one morning he got up and decided to relax and watch the morning news on TV and drink a nice cup of hot coffee.

Mrs. Jones, the school principal, heard her alarm ring but she turned it off and curled back up under the covers. When the teachers and students arrived at school the door was locked so they all turned around and went home.

At first it was just a few people who weren't doing their jobs, but soon there were more and more people who decided that they would be lazy, too!

It didn't take long for the village to start looking ramshackled and neglected. Soon the pretty little houses not only needed to be painted but the shutters started falling off, and the lawns had grown so long you couldn't see the porches!

Mr. Bailey got so behind delivering his mail the post office was piled high with letters and packages.

The shopkeepers stopped sweeping in front of their shops and only opened their doors to customers when they felt like it.

The garbage man stopped picking up the garbage so bags of trash were piling up on the sidewalks.

The school closed because the teachers were too lazy to teach and the children were too lazy to study.

The villagers got so lazy they threw their wrappers onto the streets so the whole town was covered in litter. Even the pretty little stream that flowed through the village was full of bottles and cans.

The village had become a disgrace! No longer did the villagers take pride in their town. There were many people who were upset about the changes, but finally even they gave up when they saw that nobody else seemed to care.

But there was one little girl named Lilly who did care. Lilly lived in the village and she enjoyed walking to school every morning. She loved her teacher and had fun playing with her friends at recess every day. But now the school was closed and Lilly stayed home every day.

Lilly hated staying home. Her mother tried to make her happy by reading books to her and pretending to be her teacher, but Lilly was bored. She decided that she must come up with a plan.

One morning Lilly woke up bright and early and marched into the village and went straight into the Mayor's office. "Good Morning, what can I do for you today?" he said.

"Mr. Mayor, I have an idea that will wake up the villagers and turn our village back into the prettiest village in the land."

"What is your idea? I have tried everything but this town has become so lazy they won't listen to a word I say."

"Let's have a contest," Lilly told him. "Let's get the villagers to compete to see who is the 'Most Valuable Citizen' in the village. You could announce the name of a winner and present them with a beautiful trophy at a ceremony and celebration in the town square."

The Mayor got up from his desk and walked around to shake Lilly's hand. "I think you have a great idea and I will do everything in my power to make sure this contest is a success!"

So Lilly and the Mayor's office worked together to plan. They printed flyers and delivered them to every door in the village. At first they wondered if anyone would try to compete, but little by little they noticed the villagers were starting to get back to work.

Mr. Parker painted his house and soon all of his neighbors painted their houses, too. The paint shop was so busy selling paint and brushes they had to order more to fill all of the orders.

Mr. Bailey worked overtime sorting out the mail and delivering the letters and packages that had been piled up in the post office.

Miss Bridget called a meeting of all the shopkeepers and they all agreed to start sweeping in front of their shops and keeping regular hours.

Mrs. Jones called all of the teachers and children to invite them to come back to school. They met in the school auditorium and decided that they could all do their part by picking up the litter.

Everyone started to work together and little by little the village started coming back to life. The freshly painted houses looked so pretty that their owners even mowed their lawns, painted the fences, and planted beautiful flowers.

The shopkeepers not only swept in front of their store but they washed their windows and created beautiful new window displays.

The garbage trucks buzzed up and down the streets as the workers tossed the heavy bags of trash into the trucks.

The students and their teachers picked up the litter in the parks and even waded in the stream to collect the bottles that were floating.

The Mayor did his part by encouraging everyone and telling them how proud he was of their hard work. They were happy when the Mayor took notice because of course they all wanted to win the "Most Valuable Citizen" Award.

The villagers were pleased with the work that they had done and they were proud of how beautiful the village had become. They dressed up in their best clothes and went to the village square for the ceremony to find out who the Mayor had chosen for the "Most Valuable Citizen" Award. Some of them had written their acceptance speech on a small piece of paper and had it tucked away in their pocket just in case they were the lucky winner!

The crowd hushed as the Mayor made his way up the stairs to the bandstand. Lilly and her mother and father were in the crowd and eager to hear who had won. The Mayor stepped up to the microphone and began to speak.

> I am proud of each one of you and I am thankful for all your hard work. Our village is once again the 'Prettiest' village in the land. I want to thank a special girl for giving me the idea to have a contest. It is because of her we have all done our part to bring our village back to life. Let's give a round of applause to Lilly who inspired us to work together to clean up our village.

The crowd clapped and cheered as Lilly went up the stairs of the bandstand to stand next to the Mayor.

"I know that you are all expecting me to name the winner of this beautiful trophy," he said to the crowd. "But one person alone could never have done all of the work himself. It took all of you working together to make the village beautiful again so I have awarded this trophy to everyone," he said as he waved his arm across the crowd.

The villagers looked at each other, wondering what the Mayor was saying. Then he unveiled the trophy. They gasped as they saw the names of every family engraved on the trophy. They cheered and hugged each other because they knew the Mayor was right. Each one of them had done their part, but they could never have cleaned up the whole village alone. They cheered and thanked the Mayor and Lilly for bringing the community back together.

The villagers spent the rest of the afternoon celebrating in the town square. They took turns admiring the trophy that would be proudly displayed in the town hall. They enjoyed their picnic and visited with each other while the children played games and waded in the stream.

They were having such a good time it was evening before they packed their bags to go home. They said their good-byes and as they walked back to their houses they realized that winning the trophy wasn't really what was important after all. The real prize was the joy of living and working together in the Prettiest Village in the land.

After Reading

Discussion Questions

1. Summarize the main problem of the story and tell how the problem was solved.
2. What important lessons can we learn from this story?
3. Do you think a problem like this could ever happen in your community? Explain your thinking.
4. How does this story demonstrate the Global Concept of Interdependence?
5. How does this story demonstrate the Global Concept of Change?

Charting Activity

Together with the class create a summary of the events as they occur in the story and determine the lessons the village learned.

Story Map

Name_____ Date_____

Title:

Author:

Main Character (s)

Main Events in the story:

Problem/Solution:

What Global Concept was demonstrated in the story?

What did you learn about the Global Concept _____from the story?

Figure 3.2

Closing Activity

Students will create their own Lazy Village Mini Book to show their understanding of the events in the story.

Procedure

Fold one sheet of paper in half. On the cover ask students to write the title of the story and draw a picture and captions to show how lazy the villagers had become and what the village looked like when everyone stopped doing their jobs.

On the inside pages ask students to write a summary and draw pictures with captions to show how the village changed when everyone worked together and did their jobs. Ask students to give the village a new name and label it on the inside of their book to show how the village changed after all worked together.

Give students ample time to create their Mini Book and share it with the class. Display the Mini Books in the classroom to show students' understanding of "Interdependence."

LESSON 4

Identifying Problems, Seeking Solutions, and Taking Action!

Key Standards

- **Social Studies D4.7:** Identify ways to take action to help address local, regional, and global problems.

Objective

- I can identify a problem and create a plan to solve it so I can take action to help my community.

Focus Skill: Problem/ Solution

Activity 1: Whole Group/Problem/Solution Frame

Identifying problems and seeking solutions is an important skill to teach children as they learn to look at the world using Global Concepts. Using a problem/solution frame will help students to sort their ideas as they work to come up with a plan. But the key to making positive changes in the world is to work together to take action!

Resources: Problem/Action Plan/Solution frame to be displayed on chart paper or on the smartboard; chart paper and markers for each group

Procedure

Tell students that today they are going to learn how to solve problems just like Lilly. Together with the class complete the Problem/ Solution frame using the story about the Lazy Village, using Lilly's solution as a model.

K–2 Frame

Table 3.2

Problem	Action Plan	Solution
The village became lazy and the whole place started falling apart. The shops and the schools closed, the grass and bushes grew tall, the river became polluted, and the people stopped caring about their village.	1. Lilly and the mayor started a contest to find the "Most Valuable Citizen." 2. They made flyers and posted them all over town. 3. The villagers decided to get to work!	The villagers painted their houses, mowed their lawns, and went back to work. The kids went back to school and worked with their teachers to clean up the park and the river. The town had a celebration and they all won the prize because they worked together!

3–5 Frame

Table 3.3

What is the problem?	What are the effects of the problem?	How can the problem be solved?	What action steps will help to solve the problem?	How will you know if the plan is successful?
The villagers got lazy and stopped doing their jobs and taking care of their community.	The village fell apart. Shops and the school closed. The houses needed painting and the river was polluted.	The villagers need to get back to work and take care of the village!	1. Have a contest to motivate the villagers. 2. The villagers starting taking care of their community.	1. The houses and yards are beautiful again. Shops are open. 2. The teachers and students go back to school. 3. The villagers start working together and taking pride in their community again.

Activity 2: Working Together to Solve Problems

Procedure

K–5: Whole Group Activity - Step 1

Brainstorm and Chart a list of problems in the classroom, school, and community.

K–2: Whole Group Project - Step 2

Review the chart the class created. Give each student a star and ask them to put their star on the problem that they think is the biggest problem that their class can help solve. When every child has voted, lead a discussion about why they chose the problems and determine which problem the class chose. Create a Problem/Solution frame focused on the problem they chose on chart paper and do it together with the class. See example Table 3.4.

Table 3.4

Problem	Solution	Plan
Kids bring plastic water bottles to school and throw them away. The water bottles are filling up the dumpsters.	Recycle water bottles at school.	1. Make posters to tell kids to recycle their water bottles. 2. Put a recycling tub in each classroom for plastic bottles. 3. Student volunteers pick up bottles and take them to the recycling bin outside.

3–5: Small Group Project – Step 2

Divide students into groups of no more than four. Ask each group to choose one problem from the chart. Give each group their own chart paper to draw the problem/solution frame. Students will work together to complete the problem/solution frame and create an action plan. See example Table 3.5.

Table 3.5

What is the problem?	What are the effects of the problem?	How can the problem be solved?	What action steps will help to solve the problem?	How will you know if the plan is successful?
There is too much food wasted in the cafeteria.	The money spent on the food is wasted. Food has to be thrown away. Kids are hungry because they didn't eat.	Students can help to create a menu of food they like to eat. Students should only take the amount of food they need.	A student committee should be formed to meet with school and cafeteria leaders. Committee works together to create healthy and tasty menus that the students will enjoy eating. Students in the school need to be informed about the issue and encouraged not to waste food.	Less food will be thrown away. Students will be happier with the meals. Money will not be wasted on food students don't eat.

LESSON 5

Students in Action

Objective

- I can solve problems by creating a plan and taking action.

Procedure

K–2: Review the problem/solution frame the class created. Tell students that today is the day they are going to put the plan into action! Working together in groups students will create posters to support their plan to solve the problem. The class can hang their posters and present their campaign to other classes in the school.

3–5: Each group will create a 3–5 minute presentation to share the problem they chose and their campaign with solutions and their action plan. Your class may want to choose the project they liked the best and work together as a class to put it into action!

Extension Activity

Community Service

Once you have completed the lessons on Change and Interdependence it is possible that your students will become inspired to take action! This is the time for you to think about a Service Learning Project that your class could do this year. There are many ways that your students can help to make a difference in the world that could start in your classroom. If you have done community projects in the past, or if this is your first time, don't worry! Keep the project focused and simple so your students can all participate and feel good about the work they have done!

Involve your class in making the decision to serve and let them come up with the ideas for implementing their service project. Your class may choose one of the problems you have already explored or they may come up with a different one. Use the problem/solution frame to help them to design their own unique solutions and action plan. I encourage you to keep the plan simple so you can implement it with ease.

I am listing below some service learning projects that I have seen work well in classrooms that you may be interested in trying! Some of them are very simple and will not take a lot of planning on your part; others are a bit more involved and will take class time. This is a great way to involve parents and the school community! Your community service project does not have to be complicated to be successful. Here are some ideas to get you started.

Community Service Ideas

Thanking Community Helpers: This is a great time for you to invite your community helpers to visit your classroom. Students can hear firsthand what professionals do to help keep the community safe. A great project for your class might be to write thank-you notes to the firemen and women and police officers in your neighborhood. Your class could also bake cookies to take to the station! You might even consider adopting the fire station, police headquarters, or a community service agency in your neighborhood.

Humane Society: Invite a volunteer from the Humane Society to visit your classroom. The students will love seeing a dog or cat and hearing about the services the Society provides to help animals. A great project would be to collect dog and cat food to donate to the local shelter.

Helping Senior Citizens: There is a natural connection between senior citizens and children. Children will love visiting the local senior center and the residents will enjoy spending time with the children. Your class might be able to adopt a local center and visit throughout the year to sing to the residents, play games, and read together. Children will feel good about doing nice things for the Grandmas and Grandpas at the center!

Penny Collection: I am sure there is a local charity or a school project that could use some actual cash! This is a great way for a class to contribute and make a difference in the community. Once the class has chosen a charity to raise money for ask them to bring in coins to donate. This is also a good math connection as students count the money and see the funds add up!

Playground Buddies: Work together with your students to plan a community service project to be buddies to younger students on the playground and in the school. Kindergarten and first-grade students will enjoy having a buddy to read to them, play with them, and share special activities together. This is a great way to create a "Bully Free" school environment.

Food Drive: Many schools have a food drive every year so your class will naturally have an opportunity to participate. However, did you know that food pantries need a lot of help? Ask the food pantry in your community if they could use student helpers at their location. Students can check the fresh dates on food items and stock the shelves. Not only will your students have fun, they will also provide a great service!

Additional Lesson Ideas and Resources

Create an "Interdependence" collage. Look through magazines and newspapers to find pictures that show community helpers and examples of people working together. Add pictures to the collage to create a class "Interdependence" poster.

Create an Acrostic Poem that illustrates the meaning of INTERDEPENDENCE.

I have an important role to play in the world

No one can survive on their own

To help someone else in need is our responsibility

Everybody is connected

Recycling helps our planet

Doing my best at school is one of my important jobs

Everyone is important

People depend on each other

Each person has a special role to play

Never let your family down, they depend on you!

Depending on others around the world

Even children can help the world

Not even the honeybee can live alone!

Cooperation is needed in the world

End the world's suffering by helping each other

Global Market Activity: Give students this activity as a homework assignment or a center activity. They will be amazed at how many of their favorite toys and clothes are made in other countries.

Look at the labels on your clothes, books, toys, games, and classroom equipment. Where were these items manufactured? In your Global Concepts Journal make a list of these items and write the country each was manufactured in next to it. Locate each country on a World Map or a Globe. Write a summary of your findings in your Global Concepts Journal and share with the class.

(Students may need help to see that while we depend on other countries to produce the goods we need, they are also depending on us to pay for the goods to provide them with an income to support their families.)

3–5: Small Group Project - Learning About Nonprofits

Give students an opportunity to learn about the work that agencies do to help people at home and around the world. Students can work with a small group and choose one agency to research. Give them these questions to start with and record the information they find in their Global Concepts Journal.

List of Nonprofit Agencies

The American Red Cross
The Peace Corps
UNICEF
World Wildlife Fund
Medecins Sans Frontieres (Doctors Without Borders)
Oxfam

Research Questions

1. What is their mission?
2. Who do they serve?
3. Where in the world do they help?
4. What services do they provide?
5. How are they funded?
6. Why are they needed?
7. Why do you think this agency is important?
8. How do you know that this agency is reputable?

Groups prepare a presentation to share what they learned with the class.

Big Ideas about Interdependence

- Everyone belongs to a family group, school, neighborhood, community, country, and the world.
- People in a community are interdependent.
- In a community, people play interdependent roles.
- The local community is linked to the global community.
- Relationships between human beings necessitate people forming into groups, societies, and nations.
- Ecosystems share a balance between plants, animals, and the natural environment.

Interdependence Vocabulary

Table 3.6

Family	Global Community	Relationships	Collaboration
Responsibility	Neighborhood	Habitat	Global Marketplace
Cooperation	Relationships	Local Community	Ecosystems
Import/Export	Roles	Connected	Linked

Applying the Concept of Interdependence across the Curriculum

Math: Geometry, Equations, Fact Families, Mathematical Properties

Social Studies: Community Helpers, Citizenship, Government, Societies, Economics, Trade

Science: Habitats, Ecosystems, Environmental Studies, Life Cycles

Bibliography for Global Concepts Books: INTERDEPENDENCE

The Cabbage Soup Solution (K–2)

Author: Erika Oller

Young children will enjoy this fun book about Elsie, who loves to grow vegetables on her little farm. But what happens when the cabbages start to disappear will amaze her as the animals pitch in to help her to solve the problem. In the end the whole community benefits from Elsie's vegetable garden!

I'm New Here (K–2)

Author: Anne Sibley O'Brien

Young children will love this sweet story of children from around the world who come to school in an English classroom feeling lost and afraid. But slowly they start learning words from each other, playing together, and becoming friends.

Stone Soup: An Old Tale Retold (K–3)

Author and Illustrator: Marcia Brown

Marcia Brown has taken this old tale and spun it into a fun story that showcases the Global Concept of Interdependence in a fun way. Three hungry soldiers march into a poor French village and the peasants are scrambling to feed them, but they have no food! I am sure you remember how the story goes and you will have fun sharing this with your class. Who knows, you may even want your class to make their own "Stone Soup!"

Read For Me, Mama (2–5)

Author: Vashanti Rahaman
Illustrator: Lori McElrath-Eslick

Ricardo loves going to the library to listen to books being read. He gets to take books home to read and he wants his Mama to read, but sadly, discovers that his mama never learned to read. This story shows how the community helps get Mama connected to a center where she gets a reading tutor so that she can read, too!

Home (K–5)

(U.S. version of *"Belonging"*)

Author: Jeannie Baker

A beautiful story by Jeannie Baker using her murals of an urban neighborhood to show people working together to restore their community. Interdependence is beautifully illustrated as the neighbors clean up empty lots, plant grass and trees, and paint murals to bring beauty to their home. This book shows the power that a group of people have when they work together to make positive changes in their community.

The Three Questions [Based on a Story by Leo Tolstoy] (2–5)

Author and Illustrator: Jon J Muth

A young boy learns the true lesson of Interdependence as he seeks to find the answers to three questions:

> When is the best time to do things?
> Who is the most important one?
> What is the right thing to do?

As he is seeking the answers to his questions he learns that each one of us is responsible for taking action and helping each other. The answer to the questions illustrates the basic concept of Interdependence, because helping others is the answer to the three questions.

Ruth and the Green Book (3–5)

Author: Calvin Alexander Ramsey with Gwen Strauss
Illustrator: Floyd Cooper

The realities of the Jim Crow laws are illustrated in this wonderful children's story. Ruth and her family travel from Chicago to visit her grandmother in Alabama only to discover that they aren't welcome at many diners, motels, and gas stations. Thankfully, they were given the "Green Book" that told them where they would be welcomed. The family makes it to their destination because "good black people all over the country had pitched in to help each other." This story is a great lesson in Interdependence and shows how people find ways to support each other in the face of adversity.

Culture

Who We Are and How We Live in the World

> *We may have different religions, different languages, different colored skin, but we all belong to one human race.*
>
> —*Kofi Annan*

Teaching children about Culture is the key to understanding themselves, people in their community, and people around the world. This understanding must move beyond acceptance, to truly respecting and celebrating people with traditions that are different from their own. Exploring Culture with young children is the first step to creating peace and understanding between all people in our Global World.

The World is Changing in Our Backyard

Countries around the world are seeing changes in their culture as people relocate to countries that are not their homeland. According to UNHCR, the UN Refugee Agency, there are presently 63.3 million forcibly displaced people worldwide. Of these, 21.3 million are refugees and more than half are women and children. Most of the refugees are from Syria, Afghanistan, and Somalia. It is estimated that 33,972 people a day are forced to flee their country (*Global Trends-2015*, September 18, 2016). Whether people choose to leave and move to another country by choice or are forced to relocate to a country where their family is safe, they bring their own culture and traditions with them. When people from many cultures come together communities become enriched as the population becomes more diverse, but as we know this change also brings with it many additional challenges.

President Jimmy Carter showed his understanding of the importance of culture when he said, "We become not a melting pot, but a beautiful mosaic of different people, different beliefs, different yearnings, different hopes and different dreams." The idea that people will relocate to a new country and assimilate by learning its language and customs and embracing its culture is not usually the way it happens. Immigrants and refugee families have moved around the world. It is true that they work hard to learn the language and culture of their new country, but they naturally continue to celebrate their own culture as well. When cultures come together they are more like a mosaic, or a beautiful quilt. Each square represents the culture of many different people and while the square is beautiful on its own, it is even more beautiful when all the squares are connected. As teachers we have a wonderful opportunity to create a mosaic in our classrooms by celebrating the cultures of our students and children from around the world.

Every Child Has a Story

Who are the children in your classroom? What is their story? Do you have students whose homeland is far away? Can you imagine what it might feel like to move away from your own homeland to a country with a culture that is very different from your own? You may have already experienced this so you know of the challenges families face when they emigrate. However, most people have not had this experience and may not have a real appreciation of the sacrifices and hardships people face when they leave their homeland.

When I moved to Abu Dhabi I had a similar experience. I took a position as an Education Advisor and was assigned to work in a local school to support teaching and learning. I was excited to have this opportunity and looked forward to the experience, but nothing prepared me for the Culture Shock I faced upon arrival.

I remember the nervous feeling I had as I stepped out of Customs at the Abu Dhabi Airport and was greeted by a representative from my company. We drove for miles through the desert and it was dark by the time we reached my apartment building. He carried my luggage into my apartment and showed me the four rooms that were now my new home. When he left he assured me that he would be back the next day.

The door closed and I had a sinking feeling. *Have I made the right decision to come?* Already feelings of homesickness were starting to set in. As I explored the apartment and took my suitcases into my bedroom I could feel my heart pound. I grabbed the key and ran outside only to see the lights from my window and the expanse of the Arab sky filled with stars. I went back into my apartment, made my bed, and fell into a deep sleep. Of course my story has a happy ending. I lived and worked in Abu Dhabi for two years. I fell in love with the Culture, the people, and especially the children. However, I always knew that I would be going home.

My experience and story are no comparison to the stories of refugees. Throughout my career I learned the stories of many refugee families whose children were in my classroom.

Children from Vietnam, Cambodia, and Thailand flooded our classrooms after the Vietnam War in the 70s. In the 80s we started to receive refugees from Afghanistan. Each student had a story to tell, but they came to the United States with hope in their heart. One story I remember was from a young girl of a refugee family that moved to Kalamazoo, Michigan, from Afghanistan. She had never been to school but she learned quickly. One day when we were working together at the table, she looked at me with her big brown eyes and said, "Teacher, Daddy Dead, Pow! Pow!" I remember holding her and telling her I was sorry. "Taliban kill daddy." she whispered.

Most of us cannot imagine the trauma of war and taking flight with our family to escape most-certain death. But, we can listen to our students and find out their stories. Culture is not just what we see on the outside, but it is also the experiences that people carry with them on the inside. Everybody in the world has a story and that story is part of their culture. The stories, lessons, and activities that are included in this unit will give you and your students an opportunity to hear some of these stories and also, share their own. When your students hear stories about children around the world they will not only gain understanding, but they will also feel empathy, as they learn what it feels like to "walk in someone else's shoes."

What is Culture?

"The Way of Life of a Group of People, which is learned."

Culture is the umbrella that covers all of the Global Concepts. Without an understanding of culture it is impossible to understand the world. Very simply, culture is who we are and how we live. Our culture is determined by our family and our homeland. People bring their culture with them wherever they go and this is what adds richness to countries around the world. When we begin to look at culture with young people, we learn about languages, how people dress, music and dance, food, art, and daily life at home and at school. Your classroom can become a celebration of Culture as you help children to explore the world and learn about how people live in their own communities.

Create Opportunities to Give Your Class Cultural Experiences

Enrich your Classroom with Culture

Begin the celebration by enriching your classroom environment with a collection of multicultural books and stories. Folktales from around the world, as well as modern-day stories from other countries, are a wonderful way to introduce culture through shared reading and writing activities. Artifacts, flags, and posters also add a rich multicultural feel to your classroom and give students a "hands-on" experience as they explore the world within the walls of your classroom. Listening to music from different countries and teaching children songs in different languages is also an ongoing part of multicultural education.

Guest Speakers

Invite visitors to your class to share aspects of their culture with your students. You may have a parent who is eager to share their own culture, but there are also community members who would look forward to the opportunity. When real people come into the classroom and share stories with the students about their life and experiences, students get a real glimpse into their culture.

Use Technology to Connect Your Students to the World!

Take your children to China during the Chinese New Year. Talk with students in a classroom in England, Australia, or anywhere in the world! The opportunity to talk with students around the world is now as easy as adding

Image 4.1 American Girl dolls and stories are a great resource to teach students history and culture in a fun way!

Skype to your computer. Cool websites to help you make those international connections are listed in the Resources section at the end of this chapter!

Cultural Field Trips

School trips are fun for students and can provide valuable learning experiences. Look around your community to find interesting and unique field trips for your class. Do you have a local international market? Taking your students to visit a market with a variety of international foods and international customers is a real experience. Contact the manager to arrange a tour for your class!

Is there an ethnic restaurant near your school? A field trip to a restaurant is a great way to learn about the food they eat, how it is prepared, and even how it is eaten. Cultural fairs and festivals are always a great way to introduce your class to different cultures. Take your students to a local museum to give them a glimpse of the culture of people around the world.

Celebrations

Find opportunities to celebrate with your class. Every culture observes special traditions during the holidays. If you have a diverse class, this is a perfect opportunity to invite family members to share their holiday traditions with the class. Your class will have fun learning about celebrations and traditions of people around the world. You can also have fun celebrating International Days, such as the UN Peace Day which is held every year on September 21.

Teaching Culture in Your Classroom

Teaching children about culture begins with a look at their own culture. In this unit you will find a variety of stories, lessons, and activities to choose from. The first story, "What is Culture?," teaches children how people express their culture in their daily lives. A "Culture Chart" gives students a tool to analyze their own culture and the culture of people from around the world. Creating a Culture Quilt will give students an opportunity to share their culture with the class in a creative way. Students will also have fun looking at artifacts from other cultures to discover how people live today and how they lived long ago.

The unit concludes with two animal stories to be read to KG–2 students. These stories have a common theme that all children understand; *going to school*. "Monty Goes to School" is a story about a naughty monkey that follows boys and girls to school in a small village in Malaysia. "Omar Goes to Kindergarten" is a story about a little camel that begs his parents to send him to the local Kindergarten. Students will compare and contrast the two stories and get a peek into the culture where each animal lives.

For older students, a bibliography of good books from different cultures around the world is included to give teachers a wide variety of stories to choose from, along with extension activities. Have fun with your students as you explore different cultures, ways of life, and traditions at home and around the world. Your openness and creativity is what will make this unit meaningful and fun!

LESSON 1

What is Culture?

Key Standards

- **CCRI.2:** Determine the main ideas of a text and explain how they are supported by key details, summarizing the text.

- **Social Studies-D2.Geo.K–2:** Identify some cultural and environmental characteristics of specific places.

Objective

- I can identify the main idea about culture from the text and describe ways that people express their culture in their daily life.

Focus Skill: Main Idea

Activity 1: Discussion/Charting/Written Response (Whole Group)

Resources: Chart paper, markers, Concept Card—Culture, Global Concepts Journal

Procedure

1. Ask students what they think is the meaning of the Global Concept <u>Culture</u>. Lead a discussion about Culture based on their responses and chart their ideas. After you have charted their responses show students the Concept Card for Culture and read the definition.

CULTURE

The way of life of a group of people, which is learned

Compelling Question

How does your family and community determine how you live and what you believe?

2. Continue the discussion by asking students the Compelling Question: **How do your family and community determine how you live and what you believe?** Ask students to think about how their family and community determine how they live and what they believe. Tell them that throughout this unit they are going to learn about the cultures of people around the world, but first they must examine their own culture.

Activity 2: Read Aloud Informational Text, "What is Culture?"

Procedure

Before Reading

Introduce the story, "What is Culture?" Ask students to think about how their own culture is alike and different from other cultures as they listen to the story.

During Reading

As you read the story pause when there are questions and give students an opportunity to "Turn and Talk" with their shoulder partner and share their responses.

WHAT IS CULTURE?

Can you imagine living in a world where everybody is exactly alike? Wouldn't it be funny if we all spoke the same language, dressed in the same clothing, ate the same food, and lived in houses that all look alike? What a boring world it would be!

Of course, our world is not like that! We live in different places all around the world. We wear different clothes. We eat different foods. And we even speak different languages. Children from around the world can seem to be very different from you, but guess what, in many ways you are all very much alike!

What did you have for breakfast this morning? Cereal? Eggs? Rice? Noodles? What you eat and how it is prepared and even how you eat it is part of your culture. Your family may enjoy eating traditional dishes made with food grown locally or food that comes from far away. Children around the world eat the food that their family likes to eat. What is yummy to you may be yucky to kids in other parts of the world.

Where do you live? Do you live in a big house, a small house, or an apartment building? Is your house made of brick or stone or wood or concrete? The materials your house is made of is determined by where you live in the world. Is your house white, or pink, or blue? The color of your house and how it is decorated is also part of your culture. Our home is our shelter.

What clothes are you wearing today? Are you wearing a dress, pants, or a school uniform? Are your clothes made for warmth because you live in a cold climate? Or are your clothes light and made of cotton because you live in a warm climate? The clothes you wear, what they are made of, and the style are part of your culture.

How did you greet your friends this morning when you came to school? What did you say? Shalom? Hello? Buenos dias? The language you speak is determined by your family and where you live in the world. Having a common language is important so that you can communicate with your family, your friends, and your neighbors. Some children speak many languages. Speaking more than one language will help you to communicate with many people!

Did you go to school today? Children around the world all need to learn so they can grow up and become adults who live and work in their community. Not only is it important for children to learn to read and write, but they must also learn useful skills and trades from their family and their teachers. Most children go to a school, but some children learn at home. Wherever children go to school they are learning new things every day! What we learn and where we learn it is part of our culture!

What do you like to do in your free time? Do you play games with your friends at recess? Do you sing songs and create art at school? Playing games and sports and expressing yourself through the arts is part of your culture. Children around the world have many different ways to enjoy their free time. Everybody likes to have fun!

What is your favorite holiday? The holidays you celebrate are part of your culture. Some holidays honor your country or special events in history in your local community. Some holidays are religious and celebrate your family's faith and religious beliefs. Holidays you celebrate and your family's traditions during these special times are part of your culture.

So take a look at your own culture. You might love to play soccer or basketball. Your favorite holiday might be Christmas, Rosh Hashanah, or Eid. And maybe you love to eat noodles or rice. But whatever your way of life is, remember this, children from all around the world are just like you in many ways. It is their Culture that makes them special. And it is your Culture that makes you special, too!

After Reading

Discussion Questions

1. How do people express their own culture in everyday life?
2. How does our environment influence our culture?
3. How does our family influence our culture?
4. Is one person's culture better than another?
5. Can people from different cultures live together peacefully in the world?

Together with the class chart the Main Idea of the text with supporting details.

Think/Write/Share

Distribute the Global Concepts Journals to students and ask them to head the next section of their journal, "Culture," and copy the definition and Compelling Question.

Based on the discussion and charting, ask students to write a journal entry and draw pictures to show their own understanding, thoughts, and ideas about culture.

KG–2: Write and draw a picture about one aspect of culture (food, clothing, shelter . . .).

3–5: Write a paragraph that answers the Compelling Question: *How do your family and community determine how you live and what you believe?*

Give students time to complete their journal entry and share their response with their partner.

Informational Story Map–CULTURE

Name_____ Date_____

What is the Main Idea of the story?	List the details below that support the Main Idea:

What did you learn about CULTURE from reading the story?

What new ideas do you have to add to the story?

Figure 4.1

LESSON 2

My Culture Chart

Key Standards

- **Social Studies-D2.GEO.K–2:** Identify some cultural and environmental characteristics of specific places.

Objective

- I can create a Culture Chart to show who I am and my way of life.

Focus Skill: Identifying culture

Resources: Culture Chart, markers, crayons

Procedure

1. Display the Global Concepts Culture Chart on chart paper or your smartboard.
2. Model for the class as you fill in the chart with examples from your own culture. (KG–1 students complete the chart with the teacher then go to Lesson 3 to complete a page for their Class Culture Quilt.)
3. Give each student their own Culture Chart and ask them to write and draw pictures to show their own culture on the chart.
4. Circulate and provide teacher support to students as they create their own Culture Chart. Give students ample time to complete their chart. Ask students to share their chart with their partner or in small groups.

Global Concepts Culture Chart

Table 4.1

People and Region	Food	Shelter	Clothing	Language	Education	Free-time Activities	Holidays and Celebrations

LESSON 3

Creating My Culture Quilt

Objective

- I can create my own personal Culture Quilt to show who I am and how I live in my environment.

Resources: 11″ × 13″ construction paper, markers, crayons, completed Culture Chart to use as a reference

Procedure

1. Show students examples of quilts and lead a discussion about what stories a quilt can tell about a person's life. (Bring in a quilt or show pictures of quilts from books and online.)
2. Demonstrate for students how to make their own quilt by showing them how to fold their paper to make eight equal squares.
3. Show students how each square can be designed and decorated to show one aspect of their culture. The first square is a picture of the student and his/her name to identify the owner of the quilt. Students can use their Culture Chart to give them ideas for their quilt.
4. Give students ample work time to complete their quilt. Encourage them to fill in each square and make their quilt colorful.
5. When quilts are completed give students an opportunity to share their quilt with their group.
6. Facilitate a discussion about the quilts using these questions as a guide:
   1. Are all the quilts the same? Why or why not?
   2. What makes the quilts unique?
   3. When you look at the quilts can you see how your classmates and you are alike and different?
   4. What did you learn about yourself?
   5. What did you learn about your classmates?

KG–1: Younger students may work together to create a class culture quilt. Each child can design a personal square with a picture of him- or herself and his or her family. The drawing could include favorite foods, celebrations, and free-time activities. These squares could then be put together on a bulletin board or wall to create the students' own "Class Culture Quilt."

Examples of Culture Quilt Squares:

Student Name and Picture	Favorite Food	Home	Language—Talking Cartoon
Clothing	Celebrations	School/Education	Free-time Activities

LESSON 3

Read Aloud Narrative, "Monty Goes to School"

Key Standards

- **D2.Geo.4.K–2:** Explain how weather, climate, and other environmental activities affect the culture and environmental characteristics of peoples' lives.

- **CCRL.9:** Compare and contrast the themes, settings, and plots of stories written by the same author about the same or similar characters.

Objective

- I can compare and contrast the main characters of two stories to show how their cultures are alike and different.

Focus Skill: Compare and Contrast

Grades 4 and 5: Students will compare and contrast two read-aloud books about children from different cultures that are listed in the bibliography. I recommend two stories: *The Girl Who Buried Her Dreams in a Can* by Dr. Tererai Trent and *For the Right to Learn: Malala Yousafzai's Story* by Rebecca Langston-George. These true stories are about two girls from very different cultures that both fight for their right to an education.

Activity 1: "Monty Goes to School"

Procedure

Before Reading

Tell students that over the next two days you are going to read them two stories from two different countries, Malaysia and the United Arab Emirates. Show students on a map or globe where the two countries are located. Explain to them that both countries have hot climates. Malaysia is tropical and the UAE has a desert climate. Tell them that today they are going to hear a story about two animals that live in each country and compare the culture of each animal and discover how they are alike and different! Show them the pictures of Malaysia and discuss before you begin reading.

Image 4.2 S. K. Kampong Layau is the sweet little school in Malaysia that inspired me to write the story, "Monty Goes to School."

Image 4.3 A basket of delicious Rambutan fruit that was picked from the trees in the school yard.

Image 4.4 Ms. Noreha reads stories to her students every day. Can you imagine Monty sitting with the children enjoying the story?

During Reading

As you read, pause and share your thoughts and what you notice about the culture in Malaysia. Give students an opportunity to share their thoughts and make predictions as the story develops.

MONTY GOES TO SCHOOL

Down the long winding road, through the palm plantation, there was a happy little school named "SK Kampong Layau."

The children in the village walked to the school every morning and watched the monkeys play in the branches of the tall palm trees.

The monkeys ran up and down the trunks of the trees and bounced from branch to branch as they watched the boys and girls walk to school.

One day, Monty, a mischievous little monkey, decided to follow the children to school. No one noticed him as he passed through the gate and hid in the bushes just outside the preschool building.

Monty sat quietly and listened to the happy sounds of the children. He heard them sing songs in English and Malay. Then their teacher began to read them a story.

Monty climbed up the branches of the Rambutan tree so he could look through the window. What he saw amazed him! The children sat on the carpet at the front of the classroom. Their teacher, Miss Noreha, was perched on a little stool, reading them a storybook.

While Monty listened he nibbled on the sweet Rambutan fruit and he got a little sleepy, so he curled up and took a nap. While he napped, he dreamed of a little school full of monkeys playing in the schoolyard.

When Monty woke up, he looked into the classroom window. The children were gone. He hopped down and made his way to the door and went into the classroom. Monty leaped from table to table. He opened the markers in the baskets and drew scribbles and swirls all over the tables.

Monty spotted the reading corner and ran over to the carpet to look at books. When he became tired of books he decided to put together a puzzle.

He dumped the puzzles out onto the floor and tried to put them together. Monty became very confused and the puzzle pieces got all mixed up. He decided to play with the blocks.

Monty piled the blocks into a high tower. The tower tipped over and blocks flew everywhere. As the tower came falling down Monty jumped away and hopped to the front of the classroom.

Monty noticed the big whiteboard and spotted more colorful markers. He drew scribbles in red, blue, and green all over the board. He created a beautiful masterpiece.

As Monty finished his picture he heard the sounds of children in the play yard. Quickly he escaped out the side door and hid in the bushes next to the school.

Miss Noreha led the children into the classroom. She shrieked, "Oh my, who has been in our classroom?"

The children peeked around their teacher. They started to cry. "Teacher, Teacher. Someone has been in our classroom and scribbled on the tables."

"Oh look, Teacher. Someone has been in our reading corner and messed up all the books and puzzles!"

"Oh, no, Teacher. Somebody tipped our blocks all over the floor!"

Miss Noreha was shocked. "Who could do this?" she wondered. "I must tell Mr. Fu'ad what has happened!" She called his number.

Mr. Fu'ad rushed to the classroom. When he saw the mess he put his hands on his head. "Who would do such a thing? I must go and find the intruder at once!"

Monty raced toward the gate. But just at that moment Mr. Fu'ad stepped out of the classroom and spotted him. "Come back, come back, you mischievous little monkey." He took one last flying leap and caught Monty by his tail! Poor Monty was so frightened he began to cry.

Mr. Fu'ad held Monty in his arms and took a good look at the scared little monkey. "Don't cry." He calmed Monty down and held him close. "Maybe you just want to go to school."

Monty looked up and nodded his head. Mr. Fu'ad wiped the tears from Monty's eyes. The two of them walked hand in hand back to the classroom.

The children were all seated at their tables when Mr. Fu'ad and Monty came into the classroom. "The case is solved." Mr. Fu'ad announced. "It was just a little bit of "Monkey Business!" This little monkey caused all this trouble. He wants to go to school."

Miss Noreha went to Monty and got down on her knees to speak to him. "Do you want to be in my class? I have never had a little monkey as a student before, but if you want to come we can try."

Monty put his arm around his teacher and climbed into her lap. She hugged Monty and said, "If you are going to be part of our class you need to help us to clean up this mess." Monty nodded and started to pick up markers that were scattered on the floor.

Monty and the children put away all of the books and stacked the blocks. Monty washed the board with a cloth and scrubbed all the marks off the tables. Miss Noreha helped the children put the puzzles back together.

From that day on Monty walked proudly to school with his friends wearing his new school uniform and carrying his Superhero backpack.

He loved Miss Noreha. She gave him a sticker for good behavior almost every day.

Mr. Fu'ad was very proud of Monty. He knew all along that Monty wasn't really a mischievous little monkey. He just wanted to go to school.

SK Kampong Layau is a real school in Johor, Malaysia. The school is located in a palm plantation next to the river in the small village of "Layau." The families who live there are Orang Asli and their ancestors were the first people who lived in Malaysia. Today the small fishing village is a Muslim community.

During the time I worked at the school it had fourteen teachers and that included Mr. Fu'ad who is the Head Teacher or "Guru Besar." The "GB" is in charge of the school and takes very good care of the children in the village. Miss Noreha teaches the preschool and she is well loved by her young students.

Becky Hunt

After Reading

Discussion Questions

1. What clues in the story tell us about the culture in Malaysia?
2. How does the environment in Malaysia impact the characters and setting of the story?
3. How is the school similar or different to your school?
4. What was the problem in the story? How did Mr. Fu'ad help to solve the problem?
5. Why do you think Monty wanted to go to school?

Charting Activity

Copy the Culture Chart on chart paper. Fill in the chart using the responses of the students based on evidence from the story. Tell them that they will complete the chart when they read the next story.

You can use this fun graphic organizer or a venn diagram to compare stories!

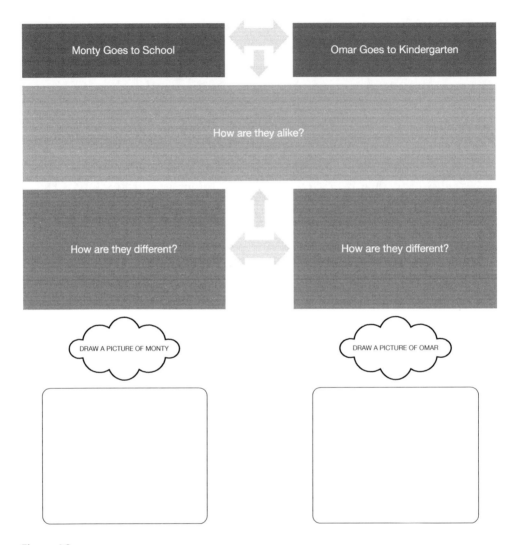

Figure 4.2

Table 4.2

Title of Story	Main Character	Setting	Food	Clothing	Shelter	School	Way of Life
Monty goes to School	Monty—a little monkey that wants to go to school.	A palm plantation in Malaysia. Very tropical and warm part of East Asia	Monty lives in a tropical climate and eats Rambutan fruit. And plays in branches of the palm trees.	Students wear a school uniform. And they carry a backpack. It is tropical so I think the clothing is lightweight cotton.	Monty lives in the palm trees. The students go to a school and live in houses in the village.	The classroom is full of fun learning activities and toys. They sing songs in two languages, English and Malay.	Monty lives with the other monkeys in the trees. The children live in the village and go to school. The people who live in the village are fishermen.

Journal Writing Activity

K–2: Ask students to pick their favorite part of the story to write about and draw an illustration to show the environment where the story took place.

3–5: Ask students to write a summary of the story and include details that show how the tropical environment impacts the daily lives of the characters in the story.

LESSON 4

Read Aloud Narrative, "Omar Goes to Kindergarten"

Before Reading

Introduce the story, "Omar Goes to Kindergarten." Remind the students that Omar lives in the desert and just like Monty he also wants to go to school. Tell them to listen to the ways that Monty and Omar are alike and different.

During Reading

Share your thinking as you read to your students and give them an opportunity to share their thoughts and ask questions throughout the story.

OMAR GOES TO KINDERGARTEN

In the desert there lived a little camel named Omar. The desert is very hot and full of sand, but believe it or not, the desert is the best place for little camels like Omar to live.

Omar could travel long distances in the desert because his footpads made it easy to walk on top of the sand. He never got thirsty because the extra fat inside his hump turned into water when he needed it. His hair protected his skin and kept him cool in the desert sun, and when the wind blew the sand into his eyes, Omar could brush it away with his long, beautiful eyelashes.

Every day Omar and his parents left the camel farm and wandered around the village to nibble on the bushes and the date palm trees. Omar often saw boys and girls waiting for the bus to take them to school, and they waved to Omar along the way.

One day Omar asked his mother a question. "Why can't I go to school, Mama?"

"Omar, little camel boys go to Camel School to learn how to run races at the racetrack."

"But I don't like to run," said Omar.

"At Camel School you will learn how to spit."

"But I think spitting is gross!"

"At Camel School they will teach you how to walk in a grand caravan."

"But I don't want to walk in a grand caravan."

Mother thought and thought. "At Camel School they will show you how to be beautiful and win the Camel Beauty Contest!"

Again Omar replied, "I don't want to be in a beauty contest."

"Omar," said Mother, "at the school in the village they teach the students to read and write and do numbers."

"That sounds wonderful!" replied Omar. "Please, Mother, just let me try!" Mother shook her head as they walked along. Omar just wasn't like the other little camels.

The next morning Mother woke Omar up very early. He got up from his cozy straw bed, stretched his legs, and took a long drink of water before he and his mother walked into town.

They didn't go their usual route but they walked to the long row of shops that lined the main street.

"Why are we going to the shops, Mama?" Omar asked his mother.

"You will see," she answered.

Omar followed his mother into the fabric shop. She ordered yards and yards of light-blue fabric. Omar stood very still while the tailor took his measurements.

They left the shop and Mother decided to reveal her surprise to Omar. "Omar, your father and I have decided to let you go to school in the village. Are you sure that is what you want?" asked Mother.

"Oh yes, Mother, more than anything." Then he rubbed his cheek on Mother's soft fur and batted his beautiful, long eyelashes. Mother gave him a nudge and a kiss as they walked toward the school.

When they arrived at school, Miss Aisha, the Principal, greeted them and agreed to let Omar start school the next day.

On their way home, they stopped by the tailor shop to pick up his uniform. Then they went to the bookshop where Mother bought Omar pencils and paper and let him pick out a new Spiderman backpack.

Omar smiled and held his head high all the way home.

The next morning, Omar woke up early and got dressed. His school uniform fit perfectly. "I'm ready!" he proudly reported to his parents.

Mother and Father walked Omar to school and kissed him goodbye at the gate. The children jumped up and down and screamed with delight when they realized that Omar was coming to school.

Omar followed the children into the gym, and Miss Aisha showed him where to line up with his class. The flag ceremony began and the students all stood in line and saluted the flag as they sang the United Arab Emirates' National Anthem in Arabic. Omar stood tall and felt so proud as he watched the flag waving.

Omar hung his backpack in his cubby and sat with the children on the carpet. His teacher introduced him. "Boys and girls, I want you to welcome Omar to our class. I know that you will be his friend and make him feel welcome at school."

The children all said hello and the teacher began their lessons for the day. Omar loved it! The teacher read them an English story and they sang the ABC song.

The morning flew by, and soon it was time for their morning break. The students ate their snacks and they all went out to play. "Hey, Omar, come play with us!" they called.

Omar had so much fun! The children raced each other and Omar took first place.

The boys competed in a spitting contest and Omar won again!

Then the children took turns riding on Omar's back around the playground until the bell rang and recess was over. The children all lined up and Omar was the first in line.

The afternoon moved by quickly and at the end of the day Mother and Father were outside the gate waiting for Omar. He chattered all the way home and told his parents all about the fun he had at school.

That evening, Mother prepared a special dinner of warm oats and date soup to celebrate Omar's first day of school. After dinner she helped Omar with his homework before she tucked him into bed.

Omar slept peacefully and dreamed about the fun he had had at school. Omar's Mother and Father also had a good night's sleep. Their little Omar was happy and that is what all parents want for their children, even if they are camels!

Nahil is a desert village that is located near Abu Dhabi in the United Arab Emirates. Camels roam about freely and are often seen alongside of the road, nibbling on the bushes and the date palm trees. The people in the village are Muslim and they are related to the ancient Bedouins that roamed the desert hundreds of years ago. The charming little kindergarten school is full of sweet little boys and girls who would be surprised if Omar came to their school!

Image 4.5 Omar and his mother walking to school in Abu Dhabi.

Image 4.6 Heidi's students love to read stories with the other children.

After Reading

Discussion Questions

1. How was Omar especially suited to live in the desert?
2. Why didn't Omar want to go to Camel School?
3. Why were Omar's parents worried about sending him to Kindergarten?
4. Why do you think Omar's parents finally let him go to Kindergarten?
5. What does this story tell you about the culture in Abu Dhabi?

Complete Culture Chart to compare the stories.

Table 4.3

Title of Story	Main Character	Setting	Food	Clothing	Shelter	School	Way of Life
Monty goes to School	Monty—a little monkey that wants to go to school.	A palm plantation in Malaysia. The climate is tropical. The school is in a small village.	Monty eats Rambutan fruit that grows on trees by the school.	He wears a school uniform and carries a backpack It is hot so the clothing is lightweight.	Monty lives in the palm trees.	The classroom is full of fun learning activities and toys. The teachers and principal care about the children. They learn Malay and English.	Monty lives with the other monkeys in the trees. The children live in the village and walk to school.
Omar Goes to Kindergarten	Omar—a little camel that wants to go to Kindergarten.	Nahil—a small village in the desert in Abu Dhabi. It is very hot in the desert.	Omar eats oats and dates and leaves off trees.	Omar wears a school uniform and he carries a backpack.	Omar lives on the Camel Farm.	The kindergarten has fun activities, a lunchroom, and games at recess. Omar has nice teachers. He learns Arabic and English.	Omar lives on the Camel Farm with his parents and goes to town every day. There are lots of shops and a tailor makes clothes.

Write/Pair/Share

K–2: Choose your favorite part of the story to write about and draw an illustration to show what happened.

3–5: Write a summary of the story and include details that show how the desert environment impacts the daily lives of the characters in the story.

LESSON 5

Comparing Cultures

Objective

- I can compare and contrast the main characters of two stories to show how their cultures are alike and different.

Resources

Culture Chart, Venn diagram, chart paper

Procedure

1. Review both stories and complete the Culture Chart with students. Make any additions and changes as directed by the students. (Figure 4.2 is for the stories above.)
2. Lead a discussion with students to find ways Monty and Omar's cultures and their stories are alike and different.
3. Put a green check on each box for things that are alike.
4. Put a red check on each box for things that are different.
5. Provide a model of a Venn diagram and show students how to use the chart to complete their diagram. *Complete the chart together for students in grades KG–2.*
6. Students or pairs of students can complete their own Venn diagram to compare the stories with a partner.
7. When students have completed the Venn diagram give them an opportunity to share their ideas in their groups.

Additional Lesson Ideas and Resources

Name that Artifact

Give your students the definition of an artifact.

Something created by humans for a practical purpose (*Merriam-Webster Dictionary*)

Play a fun game with your students. Decorate a shoebox and write on it the words, "Mystery Artifact." Tell the students that you are going to give them an opportunity to guess what the artifact is and where it came from. Put one interesting artifact in the box. Open the lid and show them the artifact. (This could be a small wooden bowl, beads, a spoon—anything that is handmade from another country.)

Ask students these questions:

1. What is the artifact made of?
2. What do the materials it is made of tell you about the region the artifact is from and the people who created it?
3. How do you think it was made?
4. What do you think it is, or was, used for?
5. Where in the world do you think this artifact is from? Why?
6. What questions do you have about the artifact?

After discussion you can reveal the true answers to the questions to your students. Locate on a map or globe where the artifact is really from!

Mystery Artifact Center Activity

Once you have played, "Name that Artifact" with your class they can have fun identifying artifacts independently. Put the **Mystery Artifact** box in the Global Concepts Center and place a variety of artifacts inside. Ask students to choose one artifact and fill out the Artifact Chart and put their name on it.

Table 4.4

Draw a picture of the artifact	What is it made of?	How was it made?	What do you think it is used for?	Where do you think it is from?

At the end of the week children share their artifact investigation sheets with the class and the teacher reveals the origin and use of the artifacts. Students will see how close they came to the correct answer!

Paper Dolls

Display books with pictures of people around the world dressed in their cultural clothing. Students can create paper dolls in clothing from different cultures using paper cutouts, felt, beads, and a variety of crafting materials. On the back of each doll they can write the name of the country the doll is from.

Cultural Kitchen Recipe Book

Ask students to make a page for a class recipe book using their family's favorite recipe. The page should include the ingredients and step-by-step directions for the recipe with a picture. This recipe can be real, or the student's idea of how to make the yummy dish!

Culture Charts

Display a variety of books about countries around the world in the Global Concepts Center. Students can choose one country and take notes about its culture, people, and important facts using the Culture Chart.

Talk Show

Display a variety of books with stories about children around the world. Give students an opportunity to choose one book to read and create a TV news show of an interview with the main character of the book. Have students develop interview questions and write their response to each one. Give students an opportunity to practice and actually conduct their interview for the class.

Applying the Concept of Culture across the Curriculum

Math: place value, reading large numbers, comparing data, reading graphs and charts

Social Studies: historical events, society, community, citizens, development of civilizations

Science: climate, scientists, inventions

Technology Links

The use of technology in the classroom has changed how we teach and how children learn so be sure to take advantage of these websites. I have reviewed many of the sites and I am recommending four that have a variety of applications, are user friendly, and are safe for you to use with students in your classroom. Please explore these sites and choose at least one to use as a focus in your Global Classroom!

Mystery Skype: Bring the world to your class through Mystery Skype. Your students will collaborate to identify where in the world the class they are skyping with is from. The game starts with Yes and No questions to begin to narrow down the areas where the class is located. Students will use their geography skills and higher-order thinking skills to solve the mystery. This also gives students an opportunity to use their listening and speaking skills! I encourage teachers of students in grades 3–5 to at least try this powerful learning experience once. I promise you your students will beg you to do it again and again! (*www.mysteryskype.com*)

Global School Network—*Linking Kids Around the World*: This website is sponsored by the United States Department of Education and will help your students to connect with the world. There are several projects that classes can become involved with, or they can even start their own. This site is also linked to the *United Nations CyberSchoolBus*, the *US Fund for UNICEF*, *Worldwide Schools*, and *People to People*. There are even online expeditions, games, and fun activities for students to explore on their own. I also like the "Guidelines for Good Global Citizens," that teach students how to be safe on the internet and show respect for people around the world. (*www.globalschoolnet.com*)

ePals: One of the sites that seems to be the easiest to use and the safest is ePals. The teacher signs up and gets the account for the class, identifies the age and grade of the students, subject focus, and special interests. Once a teacher is connected, he or she can begin to collaborate with other teachers around the world. In addition to hooking your students up with ePals, there are lessons and projects for your class to experience. There are lots of children around the world who want to practice using the language they are learning and also make friends with a student from the other side of the world! (*www.epals.com*)

Culture Quest: Nice "toolkit" of resources and classroom activities to help students and teachers deepen their understanding of culture and its meaning. (*www.culturequest.us*)

Big Ideas about Culture

1. Each individual is unique, but all people share certain similarities.
2. Culture is the way of life of a group of people that is learned.
3. Communities are made up of diverse cultures.
4. Diversity and commonality occur throughout all cultures.
5. Our culture is influenced by many cultures.
6. Everyone belongs to groups—family, school, neighborhood, community, nation, world.
7. Culture is learned.
8. Diversity of cultures, ways of life, beliefs, and values can lead to conflict.

Culture Vocabulary

Table 4.5

Traditions	Values	Citizen	Beliefs
Prejudice	Lifestyles	Religion	Environment
Artifacts	Education	Alike and Different	Celebration
Clothing	Shelter	Recreation	Language
Immigrant	Refugee	Citizen	Human Rights
Diversity	Peace	Empathy	Respect

Bibliography for Global Concepts Books: CULTURE

We All Went On Safari: A Counting Journey Through Tanzania (K–2)

Author: Laurie Krebs
Illustrator: Julia Carins

This is not your ordinary counting book! Children will be intrigued as each page turns to, "We all went on Safari . . ." The description and pictures of the animals grow in numbers from page to page showing the beauty of the land and the people of Tanzania. The book concludes with a map of Tanzania and facts about the Maasai people. You can also learn to count in Swahili!

Around the World We'll Go (K–2)

Author: Margaret Wise Brown
Illustrator: Christine Tappin

Your students will love this book as they see children from around the world shaking hands, playing together, and having fun! Use this story to help children to see that they are more alike, than different, from other children around the world.

Can You Say Peace? (K–2)

Author: Karen Katz

Celebrate the "International Day of Peace" on September 21 with this lovely book! Children from around the world wish each other "Peace" from beautifully illustrated settings of their home countries. This book lends itself nicely to a discussion with your students about peace in the classroom, in the community, and in the world!

Whoever You Are (K–2)

Author: Mem Fox

This beautifully illustrated book tells a story that weaves its way around the earth across cultures and celebrates the bonds that unite us all.

For You are a Kenyan Child (K–3)

Author: Kelly Cunnane
Illustrator: Ana Juan

Take your children into a village in Kenya to see what life is like through the eyes and experiences of a Kenyan boy. On his way to tend his grandfather's cattle he meets many wonderful people and he forgets about his grandfather's cows. He is connected to each person he meets in his small village and they each have a special role to play. This example of Interdependence gives a glimpse into the culture of a small village that will delight your students.

One Green Apple (2–5)

Author: Eve Bunting
Illustrator: Ted Lewin

Farah is a new student from a small village in a country far away. She has just arrived in America and is immersed in a culture that is very different from her own. She spends her second day of school with her new class visiting an Apple Orchard. The new experience is scary at first, but as the day goes on she makes friends with her classmates and even says her first word, "Apple." This story is a simple and beautiful illustration of how children make friends and learn from each other in their own special way.

Golden Domes and Silver Lanterns: A Muslim Book of Colors (K–5)

Author: Hena Khan
Illustrator: Mehrdokht Amini

Introduce your students to the Arab culture at home and in faraway places through this beautifully written and illustrated book. The symbols and rituals of Muslim life are presented through the rhythm of the story and the colors of the Arabic world. Keep this book in your collection for both Muslim and Non-Muslim children to enjoy.

Handa's Surprise (K–2)

Author: Eileen Browne

Handa carries a basket with seven delicious fruits inside to her friend in another village. A surprising thing happens along the way! This story takes place in Kenya and gives students a lovely glimpse into the beauty and culture of each village as Handa passes by a variety of animals.

The illustrations are beautiful! Enjoy this book with your young children and bring in some of the fruit for them to sample!

Everybody Brings Noodles
Everybody Cooks Rice
Everybody Bakes Bread
Everybody Eats Soup (K–5)

Author: Norah Dooley
Illustrator: Peter J. Thornton

These books are a wonderful way to show your students how much food is part of our culture. In each book the families learn about each other as they discover that they all eat the same foods, but just prepare them a different way. Students will enjoy the stories and can even take home the recipes and prepare these dishes with their parents to share with the class.

The Sandwich Swap (2–5)

Author: Her Majesty Rania Al Abdullah with Kelly DiPucchio
Illustrator: Tricia Tusa

Like all best friends Salma and Lily want to share everything, but NOT Peanut Butter and Jelly or Hummus Sandwiches! This story shows how culture can sometimes clash in the strangest places, like the school cafeteria! Like all young girls who squabble, Salma and Lily maintain their friendship despite their differences! What we eat is a reflection of our own cultures. This story may spark a discussion and activities related to your students' favorite foods!

Mirror (K–5)

Author/Illustrator: Jeannie Baker

Please don't overlook this amazing book! Jeannie uses her murals to compare the lives of two very different families. One family lives in Sydney, Australia, and the other lives in Morocco, North Africa. As you turn the pages of both stories you see the families doing similar activities, but in very different cultures. Take a closer look and you will see that the families are alike in many ways. There is also a clue in the pictures that links the two families together. This book will take more than one look for students to get everything they can from the pictures, so put it in your Global Concepts Center after you share it!

My Name Was Hussein (3–5)

Author: Hristo Kyuchukov
Illustrator: Allan Eitzen

This true story tells about Hussein, a Muslim boy who lived in Bulgaria after the Second World War when it fell under the rule of communists. Students will learn about the culture of this Muslim boy and feel empathy for Hussein when he and his family are forced to take Christian names. This is a powerful story that is written in a comfortable way for children to get a glimpse into the lives of a Muslim family and the oppression they faced.

The Girl Who Buried Her Dreams in a Can: A True Story (3–5)

Author: Dr. Tererai Trent
Illustrator: Jan Spivey Gilchrist

This is a true story about a young girl from Rhodesia, where education for girls was nearly impossible. She taught herself to read and write and dreamed of going to America to earn a college degree. Would her dreams ever come true?

For the Right To Learn: Malala Yousafzai's Story (4–5)

Author: Rebecca Langston-George
Illustrator: Janna Bock

The true story of Malala is one of bravery and courage. As a young girl in Pakistan living under Taliban rule she was threatened and eventually shot for going to school. Her love of learning and quest for all girls around the world to get their education has become her passion in life. Living now in Birmingham, England, Malala and her father have started an organization to fund education in countries like Pakistan. This is an important story for every teacher to share with her students.

5

Scarcity

How We Balance the Earth
and Its Resources

> *Where poverty exists there is no true freedom.*
> *—Nelson Mandela*

In Chapter 5 students will learn about the Global Concept of Scarcity. The basic needs of food, clean water, fresh air, and shelter are essential to the lives of people around the world, but as we know, not all people have what they need to live. This concept will help students to understand the difference between wants and needs and what it feels like not to have their basic needs met. This understanding will help students to learn how to have Empathy for people who are in need. This empathy is what leads us to find ways to help others. In this chapter we will explore issues of Scarcity around the world.

I will begin by sharing the story about one school that taught their students what it really feels like not to have water through day-long lessons on a "Day Without Water."

A Day Without Water

The students arrived at school and quickly noticed the official-looking signs on the drinking fountains and in the bathrooms that said, *"This water is contaminated. Drink at your own risk."* Puzzled, they came into the classrooms full of questions. "What's wrong with our water?" "What does 'contaminated' mean?" "What will we do when we are thirsty?" These are all questions that the teachers were expecting and they were prepared.

"A Day Without Water" had been planned weeks ahead by the staff at Lincoln International Studies School. We wanted our students to get a real experience and have greater understanding of the Global Concept, "Scarcity."

The day started with discussions about the problem. The teachers *weren't sure* what was wrong with the water and they told the children they shouldn't drink it. The young people seemed worried and wondered if they would be able to drink their milk at lunch (of course, we let them drink milk!). We also had a contingency plan that if they were desperate they could go to the library, which was acting as the Red Cross station for the day. The emergency workers would give them a small drink of water to help them to get through the day. Our librarian was prepared with small Dixie cups and a pail of water. "This is all the water we have and we have to make it stretch." Children got a small ration and returned to their classrooms.

Lessons were planned in every grade level that focused on water issues and shortages throughout the world. Stories were shared; statistics and lessons were all connected to the concept of Scarcity of water. At the end of the day, students were asked to write out their experience and feelings about the situation. It was a memorable day!

At the end of the day teachers all told the children the truth about the water. Discussions about what it must feel like for children around the world who don't have enough water or food became more real. Scarcity was now something that they understood and they had empathy for people around the world who face it. Throughout the month teachers continued to share stories and lessons connected to scarcity. But the Day Without Water was a day they will never forget.

Since that day there have been real issues with water in another city in Michigan. When the water in Flint, Michigan, was found to be contaminated the whole country was shocked. How long had the citizens of Flint been drinking polluted water? What will be the consequences to people's health? How will the city survive without clean water? These issues are still being addressed and it has prompted other cities in the United States to test their own water. Americans think these issues only happen in developing countries around the world, but the truth is, scarcity of clean water is an issue in many places all around the world.

Scarcity of clean water and food are just two of the issues of Scarcity that people around the world face on a daily basis. Medical care, education, and proper housing are also issues that communities struggle with as their population is growing and resources are dwindling. It is estimated that 836 million people live in extreme poverty. An overwhelming majority of people living on less than $1.25 a day belong to two regions: Southern Asia and Sub-Saharan Africa. Even in Western countries and the United States there are issues of poverty and homelessness.

The goal of this chapter is to explore the concept of Scarcity with students so they can become aware of the issues the world faces when there are shortages of basic human needs. Lessons and stories for this unit will help make the Global Concept of Scarcity real to students. This awareness will also help children to develop Empathy for people in need. The Global Concept of Scarcity must be presented to children in a way that not only shows them the inequities in the world, but also hope for the future.

The United Nations' "Global Goals for Sustainable Development" will be introduced to students to give them a broad perspective of what is being done to help people around the world. Each goal has recent data and explanations of the issues and also the plans to meet each goal. Classrooms may choose one goal that they want to support and work together to find ways that they can help. This program and its awesome website will be a key tool to teachers as they explore not only Scarcity issues, but human rights issues around the world. It is packed full of lessons for teachers, videos, and ideas for classrooms to support each goal. (*www.globalgoals.org*)

Global Goals

1. No Poverty

2. Zero Hunger

3. Good Health and Well-Being

4. Quality Education

5. Gender Equity

6. Clean Water and Sanitation

7. Affordable and Clean Energy

8. Decent Work and Economic Growth

9. Industry, Innovation, and Infrastructure

10. Reduced Inequalities

11. Sustainable Cities and Communities

12. Responsible Consumption and Production

13. Climate Action

14. Life Below Water

15. Life on Land

16. Peace, Justice, and Strong Institutions

17. Partnerships for the Goals

LESSON 1

Scarcity . . . sometimes there's just not enough!

Key Standards

- **Social Studies: D2.Eco.1.K–2**—Explain how Scarcity necessitates decision making.

Objective

- I can work together with my class to make decisions to solve scarcity issues.

Focus Skill: Problem solving and decision making

Activity 1: What is Scarcity?

Procedure

Ask students what they think the word Scarcity means. Chart their ideas and ask for examples. Tell them that the next Global Concept they are going to learn is Scarcity. Give them the definition of Scarcity and share the Global Concept Card.

SCARCITY

Balancing human needs and wants with the earth's resources

Compelling Question

How does scarcity impact our lives and the decisions we make?

Ask students why the word "balance" is in the definition. What happens when anything becomes unbalanced? This is a perfect way to think of Scarcity. When we don't have enough of what we need the world becomes unbalanced.

Math Connection: Use a real balance scale to demonstrate the meaning of balance/imbalance to help students to understand the concept of balancing the earth's resources with human needs.

Compelling Question and Discussion

Pose the Compelling Question to the class and facilitate a discussion using their thoughts and ideas about the question. Create a chart to record their ideas.

How does scarcity impact our lives and the decisions we make?

Pose a variety of scenarios about Scarcity to students and ask them to think about what the impact of the shortage would be and what decisions would have to be made as a result.

Here are a few examples:

K–2

1. There are only four swings on the playground.
2. The class has 22 students but only 12 math books.
3. You win four tickets to the movie, but there are six people in your family and they all want to go!

3–5

1. A storm hits the community and there is no electricity.
2. A manufacturing plant closes and many people lose their jobs.
3. Drinking water is contaminated.

Activity 2: Musical Chairs

Procedure

K–5

Arrange chairs in a circle so that every child has a spot. Play music while children circle around the chairs. Stop the music and give a chance for every student to sit down. Explain to them that you will remove a chair each time to create a Scarcity. Play the music and stop it; continue until there is only one chair left. Explain to the children that this is what it is like when resources disappear. As the resources disappear more and more people's needs are not being met.

Follow-Up Discussion

How did it feel when you could see that the chairs were disappearing?

What did you try to do when you realized you might not get a chair?

How did it feel when you didn't get a chair?

What did we learn about Scarcity by playing the game of musical chairs?

Closure: Tell students that Musical Chairs is fun, but in real life Scarcity issues are no fun!

Activity 3: There's not enough!

Resources

Food and/or drinks to distribute to half the class

Procedure

1. Tell the class that you brought in a treat for them today. Ask them not to touch their treat until everyone has been served. While they're seated at their desks distribute all that you brought to the students. Give one or two students several of the food items and then a few more students just get one. As you are passing them out you might think out loud, "I am a little worried I didn't bring enough . . ."

2. Explain to the students that there just wasn't enough to go around so you just gave things out the way you thought they should be divided.

3. Ask students if they think this is fair. Tell them that this is the way it works with Scarcity issues; it is not fair when some people have a lot and others have nothing.

4. Ask students to brainstorm ways you could have divided the items. *You want them to see that when there is not enough to go around decisions must be made to balance human needs with available resources. You also want them to see that some solutions might discriminate people based on gender, race, size, popularity, and so forth.*

5. Listen to the children's ideas; let them choose the best solution by conducting an informal vote (students share; someone sacrifices; and so on).

6. Stop the lesson and tell them they have just experienced a problem that people around the world have every day. There are scarcities all over the world and they impact how people live. Let them know that just like they solved their problem, they may be able to help the world solve a problem by seeking a solution and taking action.

7. Finally, give everyone the treat!

Closing Activity: Write/Pair/Share

Reflection and Journal Writing: Give students an opportunity to begin the section in their Global Concepts Journal for Scarcity by copying the definition and the Compelling Question.

KG–2: With teacher support write a story and draw a picture to show examples of Scarcity.

3–5: Write your own definition of Scarcity and give examples of scarcity issues that happen at home, in the community, and in the world.

Give students ample time to complete their journal entry and share with a partner.

Shared Reading—Informational Text, "Scarcity . . . Sometimes There's Just Not Enough!"

Key Standard

- **CCR1.2:** Determine main idea of the text, recount the key details, and explain how those details support the main idea.

Objective

- I can determine the main idea about Scarcity and list key details that support it.

Focus Skill: Main Idea and Detail

Procedure

Before Reading

Ask students to listen to the story and think about what they feel the difference is between what they really want and what they really need!

During Reading

As you read, share your thinking and reflect on some scarcity issues mentioned in the story. Give students an opportunity to share their thoughts and ask questions, too!

SCARCITY . . . SOMETIMES, THERE'S JUST NOT ENOUGH!

Think of a time when you wanted something really, really badly. You thought about it every day, you dreamed about it, you talked about it with everyone who would listen, but your mom said, "NO!" How did you feel about that? Were you mad? Were you sad? I bet you were both!

We have all had the experience of wanting something and not being able to get it. Maybe there wasn't enough money, maybe it wasn't something our parents thought was important, maybe it was just not available. Whatever the reason, it is tough not being able to get what you want.

But wait a minute! We are talking about something you want, *hmmmmmm.* What does that tell us? Oh yes, it is something you want but you don't really need. Your mom said it, didn't she, "You don't need that bike, or toy, or new electronic gadget!" And when you thought about it you knew she was right.

We all know what it is like not to get what we want, but have you ever not been able to get what you need? What if you didn't have enough food to eat or clean water to drink? Now that would be a problem, wouldn't it? There is a big difference between "Wants" and "Needs." Food, clean water, shelter, medical care, education, and family are some very important needs that all people share. You can't live without your needs being met, but you can get along just fine without the things that you want!

The truth is there are people around the world who don't have their basic needs met. How do you feel when you are thirsty? Some families live in regions where there is a shortage of water. Children and their parents have to walk miles to a well to get fresh water every day. How do you feel when you are hungry? It's no fun, is it; yet there are children in the world who don't have enough good food to eat. These are just some of the Scarcity-related issues in the world.

You might be wondering why there isn't enough for everyone. There are many causes of Scarcity. Think about it, when there isn't enough rain there is no water to drink and crops can't grow. When a storm comes it can destroy crops, tear down houses, and flood the land. When there is a blizzard it may be impossible for supplies to be transported. The shelves in the grocery stores empty fast and shortages occur. These natural disasters create Scarcity issues that people face all around the world.

But guess what, poverty is one of the biggest causes of Scarcity. When a family has limited income it is difficult to keep food on the table and a roof over their head. There are 836 million people living in poverty throughout the world. But it is not just people on the other side of the world who face Scarcity issues; there are families that live in poverty right in your community.

So the next time you think you need fancy athletic shoes, a new toy, or the latest technology take a moment to think about what's really important. Reach out a helping hand to someone in need. Look around and see what you can do to help your community. Even you can help solve Scarcity issues at home, in your community, and in the world!

After Reading

Discussion Questions

1. What is the difference between a "Want" and a "Need?"
2. How does Scarcity impact how people live and the decisions they make?
3. What causes Scarcity in the world? How do you know?
4. What Scarcity issues do you see in your community?
5. Summarize the main idea and supporting details.

Charting Activity

Together with students, write the main idea of the story and list the key details from the text that support the main idea.

Title: Scarcity . . . Sometimes, There's Just Not Enough

Main Idea:

People in the world have the same basic needs. When these needs aren't met there becomes a Scarcity. Poverty is one of the biggest causes of Scarcity issues in the world.

Key Details:

1. Food, clean water, shelter, medical care, education, and family are some very important needs that all people share.
2. There are people around the world who don't have their basic needs met.
3. There are 836 million people living in poverty today.
4. Some families in the poorest areas of Asia and Africa live on $1.25 a day.
5. You can't live without your needs being met, but you can get along just fine without the things that you want.

You may use the informational story map for Scarcity as found in Figure 5.1 and Appendix 7.

Informational Story Map–SCARCITY	
Name_____ Date_____	

What is the Main Idea of the story?	List the details below that support the Main Idea:

What did you learn about SCARCITY from reading the story?

What new ideas do you have to add to the story?

Figure 5.1

Closing Activity: Wants and Needs Collage

Procedure

In small groups ask students to work together to create their own collage to illustrate the difference between Wants and Needs. Show them an example of a T-chart labeled Wants/Needs. Give each group chart paper, magazines, glue, and markers to create their Wants and Needs collage poster. Display the posters in your classroom as a reminder of the Global Concept of Scarcity.

LESSON 3

Shared Reading—Narrative, "A Home for Lucky"

Key Standards

- **CCRL.3:** Describe characters, setting, and major events in a story using key details.

Objective

- I can describe the characters, setting, and events in "A Home for Lucky" to show how the Global Concept, "Scarcity," is demonstrated in the story.

Focus Skill: Story Structure

Procedure

Before Reading

Ask students if there has ever been a time that their family has had to make a hard decision because there was not enough money? Tell them to listen to the story "A Home for Lucky" to hear what decisions Sadie's family had to make and how their lives changed as a result.

During Reading

Read the story and pause from time to time to ask students to reflect on the actions and the feelings of the main characters and to also make predictions.

A HOME FOR LUCKY

Early morning was the time that the streets of Chicago were empty. Everyone had gone home to bed. The houses were dark and the curtains closed. The only car out belonged to the early morning newspaper delivery man making his way into the neighborhoods.

Mr. Daniels was one of those early morning people who made his stops on the street corners of Chicago. No one in the neighborhood knew he visited them each night, but he did. Ever since Mr. Daniels was laid off from his construction job he'd been out of work. The bills started piling up and he and his daughter, Sadie, moved in with his mother. It was a tough situation but he knew they'd get through it somehow. Picking up the night shift delivering the papers helped to keep food on the table.

One night Mr. Daniels took Sadie to help him make his deliveries. It was a bit of an adventure to go out so late at night and Sadie often begged to go with him, and secretly, Mr. Daniels appreciated the company.

Why he let her come on this night was a puzzle but the truth was he couldn't resist her big, brown eyes and sweet, little face. He helped her to get on her coat and mittens and they braved the cold as they made their way to the car.

The winds of Lake Michigan were blowing and snow was falling at a fast pace. Mr. Daniels knew that driving would be a challenge. As they made their way into the snowy streets they finally came to the corners where he would lay the stacks of papers that were neatly tied with a sturdy twine and covered with plastic to keep them dry.

At each stop Mr. Daniels would park the car, pop the trunk, and jump out to unload the papers over and over until the trunk was empty. It was brutal as he trudged through the snow with the chill of the wind blowing against him as he carried each heavy stack. One by one he was making progress and his route was almost completed.

Sadie enjoyed riding along and she stayed in the warm car while her father made his deliveries. They shared a thermos of hot chocolate and cookies that grandma baked. Sadie was getting sleepy as she watched out the car window. At the very last stop Sadie noticed something moving under the bushes near the streetlight.

She jumped out of the car and went to look and discovered a very cold, little kitten.

"Sadie, get back in the car," her father ordered.

"Okay, Daddy," she said as she reached under the bush to grab the kitten and she stuffed the poor little thing inside her warm coat.

Nervously, she rode along as her dad sang with the radio. Hopefully, he wouldn't notice that mysterious little bulge in her coat. The road conditions heading home were dangerous as they wound slowly through the streets filled with ice and snow. When they arrived Sadie and the kitten had fallen asleep and Mr. Daniels carried them into the house.

As he entered the kitchen he heard a very soft and muffled meow. He was suspicious, but he couldn't imagine that there was a kitten in the kitchen. Holding Sadie on his lap, he began to unbutton her coat when out poked the head of the tiny white kitten. "Well I'll be . . ." he said as he rubbed the kitten on the little black streak of hair between his tiny ears. "So, it was you I heard!"

Sleepy Sadie woke up and she quickly tried to tuck the kitten back into her coat so that her father wouldn't see. "It's too late for that, Sadie," her father said. "I have already discovered your little secret."

She picked up the poor little kitty and held him close to her cheeks. The kitten started to purr and pushed his face across Sadie's cheek. "Please, Daddy. Can we keep him?"

Mr. Daniels looked at his daughter's sweet face and said, "Yes, we can keep him and we will call him Lucky, because he was so lucky to find you on such a cold winter night."

"It looks to me like he might be hungry," he said, as he got a little saucer out of the cupboard, reached into the refrigerator, and poured out a little milk. Sadie put the kitten down and they watched him as he lapped up the milk with his little pink tongue.

"Thank you, Daddy for letting me keep Lucky. I think Grandma is going to be a little mad when she finds out in the morning."

"She will be OK with it, Sadie. I know it's been tough for you since I lost my job, but we will get back on our feet again. This little kitten needed a home, too. We can add one more little mouth to feed. Don't you worry about that!"

Lucky finished his milk and Sadie hugged her daddy and the tiny purring kitten as he carried them both up to bed. Mr. Daniels tucked her in and Lucky curled up into a ball in Sadie's arms.

As he bent down to give his little girl a goodnight kiss he watched as she fell peacefully back asleep. Looking at her one last time before he turned off the light and closed the door he smiled; it wasn't just the kitten that was lucky, but he was the luckiest one of all.

After Reading

Discussion Questions

1. How did losing his job impact the decisions Mr. Daniels had to make for his family?
2. How does this story demonstrate the Global Concept of "Scarcity?"
3. What kind of man was Mr. Daniels? How do you know?
4. Why did Mr. Daniels think he was the luckiest one of all?

Charting Activity

Chart a story map with the students. Figure 5.2 is a story map template you can use or adapt.

Closing Activity: Global Concepts Journal Response

Write/Pair/Share

K–2: With teacher support draw pictures and describe your favorite part of the story.

3–5: Write a response to the Compelling Question: *How does Scarcity impact our lives and the decisions we make?*

Give students ample time to prepare their response and share it with a partner or in a small group.

Story Map–A Home for Lucky

Name_____ Date_____

Main Characters	Setting of Story

Main Events in the story	Problem/Solution

How was the Global Concept, SCARCITY, demonstrated in the story?

What did you learn about SCARCITY from reading the story?

Figure 5.2

Introducing Global Goals

Key Standards

- **D4.7.K–2:** Identify ways to take action to help address Local, Regional, and Global problems.

- **D4.8.K–2:** Use listening and consensus building and voting procedures to decide on and take actions in the classroom.

Objective

- I can work together with my classmates to choose a Global Goal and create a campaign to raise awareness and provide support to help the goal to be met by 2030.

Focus Skills: Consensus building, planning, and teamwork

Resources

www.globalgoals.org

Procedure: Introducing Global Goals

1. Ask students to think about any ideas that they might have to help people in the world who are hungry or don't have water. Give students an opportunity to share their ideas and encourage them to be creative with their thinking.
2. Tell students that there is one organization that has come up with 17 Global Goals to help people around the world. That organization is the United Nations, and 193 countries are all working together to solve problems of Scarcity. These goals are to be met by 2030.
3. Pull up the website *www.globalgoals.org* and share it with the students. Read and review the highlights of each of the goals.
4. Go to the School tab and open "Introducing Global Goals." Share the video, "***Malala*** Introducing the World's Largest Lesson".

Think/Pair/Share

Give students one minute to think quietly about the video and be ready to answer the question: **What is the world's largest lesson?** After one minute ask them to discuss the answer to the question with their shoulder partner. Move throughout the group and listen to the students' conversations. Close this activity by sharing some of the responses and insights that you heard from the students.

Activity 2:

Share the video, "The World's Largest Lesson, Pt 2," with students. Discuss the video and tell your students that they will have an opportunity to choose one goal they feel strongly about to work together with their team to create a plan to support that goal.

Procedure

KG–2 (Whole Group): Together with the class students will vote and choose one Global Goal. With teacher support the class will explore the goals and chart facts from the website. Students will create posters to provide information about the goal they chose to support.

4–5(Small Group): Working in small groups, ask students to choose one goal that they want to support. Together they can explore the goal on the website and gather research for a presentation. Students will develop a plan and create a campaign to persuade people to help support the goal.

Closing Activity: Presentations

Give students ample time to complete their projects and prepare for their presentations. KG–2 students can share their posters with the class and tell what they learned about the goal. Grades 3–5 can present their Global Goal and support plan to the class to persuade students to join their group!

Additional Lessons and Resources

Economic Lesson: Budget Activity

KG–2: Provide students with the grocery flyer from a local store. Give students a budget to spend and ask them to add up the prices of the items they chose. If they don't have enough money in their budget they must make a choice and cross some items off their list! Tell them that everyone has a budget and when you don't have enough money to buy what you want, you must only buy what you need!

3–5: It is surprising to students to find out how much things actually cost and how much of a family's budget goes to housing and food and basic necessities. Provide students with a monthly salary and ask them to prepare a budget for a family of four. Provide newspapers and access to the Internet to find an apartment, purchase a car, and buy groceries for the month.

Hunger in your community

3–5: Give students the opportunity to research the need for food in your community and identify agencies that help people in need. Choose one agency to support and contact them to determine how your class can help. A class- or school-wide food drive is always a good way to start but there might even be more that you can do. Think about actually visiting a food bank to help check fresh dates and stock shelves. If it is not possible to visit a food bank invite a community leader to come and speak to your class about the work they do to help people in need.

You have already taken a look at the Global Goals with your class and enjoyed the introductory activity. Spend time looking at the lessons that have been created for each goal. There are fabulous resources that you will want to use to continue as your class learns more about the Global Goals. Posters, lessons, books, and videos are free to teachers around the world to use with their class. Once your students are introduced to the goals they will want to become involved in one of the projects. There are many projects specifically designed for students and they are all listed in the School section of the website. Help your students to make a difference and feel good about themselves through one of these worthwhile organizations.

Big Ideas about Scarcity

- The most basic economic problem is Scarcity.
- Societies have a given amount of labor, capital, and natural resources.
- People's wants for goods and services are often greater than what can be produced.

- Choices must be made when Scarcity exists.
- There is enough for everyone, but not everyone has equal and fair access to goods and services.
- Resources are limited and tied to the environment.
- People and society are responsible for conserving the earth's resources.
- Poverty is a major factor impacting Scarcity throughout the world.
- Global Warming is creating Scarcity issues in the world and changing our environment.

Scarcity Vocabulary

Table 5.1

Wants and Needs	Natural Resources	Non-Renewable Resources	Choices
Economy	Consumer	Supply and Demand	Reduce
Recycle	Poverty	Distribution of Goods	Sustainability
Human Rights	Reuse	Shortage	Community Service

Applying the Concept of Scarcity across the Curriculum

Math: place value, money/currency

Science: climate change, global warming, ecology, pollution, natural resources, drought

Economics: supply and demand, consumerism

Social Studies: geography, population, climate, global production of goods, distribution of goods, history

Bibliography

If The World Were a Village
A Book about the People (K–5)

Author: Davis J Smith
Illustrator: Shelagh Armstrong

This informational text is a valuable resource for all ages as students begin to learn about our Global Village. The increase of populations and lack of available resources is evident as the Global Village grows. Use this book as a reference when you are teaching children to understand Scarcity. This book also lends itself to great math lessons as students learn to read and compare numbers. In addition, David Smith has included an article at the end of the book full of great ideas for teaching children about the global village. (Make sure you have the most recent edition for the most up-to-date statistics and facts!)

The following books are beautiful stories about our basic needs; food, water, and shelter. Enjoy reading them with your class!

Last Stop on Market Street (K–3)

Author: Matt De La Peña
Illustrator: Christian Robinson

The Caldecott Honor, John Newberry Medal, and the Coretta Scott King Award have all been awarded to this beautifully written book about a young boy who rides the bus to a Soup Kitchen after church on Sunday. What is surprising is the colorful friends he and his Nana meet along the way and what they actually do at the Soup Kitchen. Nana teaches important lessons along the way that every child needs to hear. *This book should be number one on your Read Aloud list!*

It Could Always Be Worse (K–3)

Author: Margot Zemach

Your students will love hearing you read this Yiddish folktale about a poor unfortunate man that lived with his mother, his wife, and his six children in a little one-room hut. It was so crowded and noisy he couldn't take it anymore. He went to the Rabbi to get advice, and the advice he gets is both surprising and delightful! Have fun with this story as children get a firsthand look at the realities of scarcity with a little bit of Jewish culture thrown in for fun!

A Bucket of Blessings (K–3)

Authors: Kabir Sehgal and Surishtha Sehgal
Illustrator: Jing Jing Tsong

Water is one of our basic needs and this story is an old, old Indian folktale about a monkey who lives in a jungle and it hasn't rained for weeks. He remembers a story his mama used to tell him about how peacocks can make it rain by dancing. His quest for the peacock and finally water is a beautiful story that not only engages children but shows them the importance of water. The proceeds to this book go to charity: water. You can learn more at www.charitywater.org. Have fun with this story, the children will love it and it would be a great story for children to perform as a play or puppet show.

The Water Princess (2–5)

Author: Susan Verde
Illustrator: Peter H. Reynolds

Walking to get water every day with her mother is a ritual that Gie Gie endures as a matter of survival. Her small village is a long way from water, but for the family to survive they must fill their pots with water and carry them back home. Gie Gie throws a fit, pretends she is a princess, and tries to command the water to appear, but it doesn't help, or does it?

Home (K–5)

Author: Carson Ellis

Everyone needs "shelter" and this book is full of beautiful illustrations of homes around the world and in our imagination. Children will see that all homes provide shelter, but not all homes are the same! *Home* would be a wonderful read-aloud for young children to inspire them to draw a picture of their own shelters, or one in their imaginary world!

A Chair for My Mother (K–3)

Un Sillon Para Mi Mama
Author: Vera B. Williams

Here is another Caldecott Honor Book that you will want to share with your students. Mama works hard as a waitress in a diner and her old chair was destroyed by fire. Her little girl saves coins in a jar to save up enough money to buy her mama a new chair. This story is sweet and shows how even when a family hits tough times they can work together and survive.

Coming On Home Soon (3–5)

Author: Jacqueline Woodson
Illustrator: E.B. Lewis

G.P. Putnam's Sons; a division of Penguin Young Readers Group
This beautifully illustrated story takes place during wartime when some women had to leave their families to work in the city while the men were off fighting the war. Ada Ruth has to say Goodbye to her mama and endure the time that passes without her. Not only does this story demonstrate the Global Concept, Scarcity, but it also shows the changes that happen when families are forced to take drastic measures to make ends meet.

One Hen: How One Small Loan Made A Big Difference (2–5)

Author: Kate Smith Milway
Illustrator: Eugene Fernandes

Kojo and his mother live in a little mud house in Ghana and there is never enough money or food to eat. This all changes when his mother gets a small loan to give her money to start a small business. She buys a cart and with a few coins that are left Kojo buys a hen. This one little hen starts a business that not only helps Kojo and his mother, but grows into a business that brings food and jobs to Ghana. Students will enjoy this story and also learn an important lesson about hard work and entrepreneurship!

Beatrice's Goat (2–5)

Author: Page McBrier
Illustrator: Lori Lohstoeter

Beatrice's family lives in Uganda and they receive a wonderful gift from Heifer International, a goat. Not only does the family now have milk to drink, but that little goat also gives Beatrice an opportunity to go to school. Your class may want to learn more about Heifer International and raise funds to donate so that they can help families just like Beatrice's!

Four Feet, Two Sandals (2–5)

Authors: Karen Lynn Williams and Khadra Mohammed
Illustrator: Doug Chayka

This beautiful story gives us a glimpse into the lives of people living in refugee camps. The reality of living in tents with limited resources comes to life when two young girls each get one new sandal. They decide to share the sandals and their friendship grows. This story is set in one of the largest refugee camps in Peshawar, along the Afghanistan-Pakistan border.

Ada's Violin: The Story of the Recycled Orchestra of Paraguay (3–5)

Author: Susan Hood
Illustrator: Sally Wern Comport

Our students couldn't imagine what it would be like to live in a garbage dump, but that is exactly where Ada Rios grew up. The concept of Scarcity is illustrated here to show what life is like to people who live in extreme poverty. But one thing that Ada's family has that no one can put a price on is music. Ada develops a love for music and her grandmother signs her up for violin lessons. There is only one problem; there aren't enough violins for the students to play. The problem is solved when her teacher begins to recycle scraps from the dump to make violins for the children. This story of the Recycled Orchestra is true and they have performed for large audiences throughout the world.

6

Power

The Ability to Control Something
or Someone Else

> *Let us pick up our books and pencils. They are our most powerful weapon.*
>
> —*Malala Yousafzai*

In Chapter 6 students will explore the concept of Power and begin to see that they have power to make a difference in the world. The final story and lessons lead to the concept of peace where classrooms and schools are challenged to create their own "Peace Club."

Power is the final Global Concept that we introduce because it has such impact on every aspect of our lives and our world. We are taught to respect power and we are in awe of power. Whether we are looking at people in power, world powers, or the power of nature we are looking at a force and the impact it has on our world.

But how do we teach young people to understand not only the power in this world, but also the power within themselves? It is our job as Educators to empower our students so that they can make a positive impact on our world. Power is the force that provides each one of us the ability to act, to make changes, and to impact our lives and our world. It is how we use that power that makes all the difference.

"Mother May I?"

Do you remember playing this game as a child? It is simple; one child is "mother" and the rest of the children line up in a row, facing mother. "Mother May I?" we asked, and the all-powerful *mother* would either grant us permission or send us back to start. Mother had all the power; we had none.

I think about this game now and realize that it provides us with a great opportunity to teach children what it feels to be powerful and what it means to be powerless. There was no question that having the power felt good. Mother could determine the fate of each child in the line and she used her power at random.

Sometimes mother seemed to play favorites. Mother, seemingly a dictator, answered to no one. The game often ended with a group of children chasing Mother away and replacing her with someone else who we thought might use their power more fairly. Playing "Mother May I?" is a great way to get children to start thinking about the concept of Power and this game will be included in Lesson 1.

The definition of Power is *"the ability to control something or someone else."* It is the struggle between power and control that creates conflicts in relationships at home and in the world. It is the balance of the power in nature that controls our weather systems, our climate, our oceans, and our heavens. But of course people have power, too. Children learn that they have power the day they are born. From the time a child is a baby they have had the ability to get their wants and their needs met. Crying and tears are powerful and parents are trained early on to take care of their baby's needs so the crying will stop. This lesson is learned early and develops as a child grows. Using power to "get" something is a child's first experience with power, but eventually children learn to use their power to make good decisions and do the right thing.

The concept of power is seen daily in the classroom and throughout the school. Students learn to respect the authority of the principals, teachers, and staff that help them throughout the day. They learn the routines and rules that are put into place to help to make the school day go smoothly. Power is also played out by children as they use their brainpower to learn and make decisions. Throughout the day everyone uses the power of their heart as they share empathy with others and reach out their hand to someone in need.

When children learn to look at conflicts through the lens of the Global Concept of Power, they bring new understanding issues. Bullies try to take power away from others and control them with threats of violence, name calling, and exclusion. The study of leaders who have made impact on the world can be examined as children begin to look at how they used their power to make both positive and negative impact on the world. Historically power has been used to take control of nations and changed the lives of people throughout the world. Students will have greater understanding of world conflict once they understand the concept of Power. This understanding will bring lessons to deeper understanding as children begin to think about how power is used in their own lives and in the world.

Teaching children the concept of Power will help them to see that power can be both a negative and a positive force and it is how they use their power that makes a difference. Ultimately we want children to develop into Global Citizens that look beyond themselves and use their power to help others. Helping children to find their voice and use their inner power to make the world a better place is one of the important goals of this chapter.

LESSON 1

Introduction to Power

Key Standard

* **CCRI.2:** Determine the main ideas of a text and explain how they are supported by key details.

Objective

* I can determine the main ideas about Power and explain how they are supported by details from the text.

Focus Skill: Main Idea

Activity 1: Introduction to Power

Procedure

Ask students to think about the meaning of the word <u>Power</u>. Invite them to share their definition and examples of power. Chart their responses. Share the Concept Card with students and together compare their definition to the one on the card.

POWER

The ability to control something or someone else

Compelling Question

How can people use their power to make the world a better place?

Activity 2: Mother May I?

Procedure

Introduce the game "Mother May I?" to the class by telling the students that they are going to play a game that illustrates Power in a fun way. Explain to them how the game is played and tell them that only MOTHER has power!

Mother May I

There are many versions—here is one simple way to play!

Number of players: 3–10

Roles: One mother and the rest are her children.

How to play: Children line up in a row. Mother takes 20 steps back and faces her children. One by one the children ask for permission to take steps toward Mother. They must say, "Mother May I . . ." Children can ask to take baby steps, giant steps, bunny hops, and so on. They must be strategic to get Mother to say "Yes." If they ask for too many steps she will most likely say no! Mother's response must be "Yes; No; You may take three baby steps" or whatever the child asked for.

Rules: Children take turns asking Mother for permission to take steps forward.

Children must say, "Mother May I?"

If a child doesn't say, "Mother May I?" they are automatically denied permission.

Mother has the authority to give and deny permission to children. If children are denied they must return to the line.

How to win: The child that gets close enough to touch Mother is the winner. The winner then gets a turn to be the mother.

Let the rest of the class observe and give others a chance to play if time allows.

Wrap-Up and Discussion

After your class has had fun with this game bring them to the carpet and lead a discussion of Power and the "Mother May I?" game.

Discussion Questions

1. Was it fair that Mother had all the power? Why or why not?
2. Did Mother use her power fairly?

3. How did it feel to be a child? The mother?
4. How does this game illustrate the Global Concept of Power?
5. How is this game sometimes like real life?

Activity 2: Read Aloud—Informational Text, "Who Has the Power?"

Procedure

Before Reading

Tell students that you are going to read them a passage to help them to learn more about the Global Concept of Power. Ask students to listen for all of the different kinds of power that are mentioned in the passage.

During Reading

As you read the story pause to give students an opportunity to respond or ask questions about Power as it is introduced throughout the text.

WHO HAS THE POWER?

What do you think of when you hear the word *Power*? Do you see Superheroes saving the world from disaster? Do you imagine a powerful storm with raging winds and driving rain? Or maybe you think of the power of a strong leader, like the president, or a king! Whatever you think of when you hear the word *power*, it is most likely correct, because there are many kinds of power in the world.

The power of nature is one of the first things most people think of when they hear the word *power*. Nature is powerful and unpredictable. Weather forecasters do their best to let us know us when a storm is coming so that we can prepare, but sometimes we don't get much of a warning. Suddenly you hear thunder in the distance, lightning flashes, and you run for shelter! The power of a storm can take down trees and even cause fires and floods.

The power of nature also causes the movement of the earth, the planets, the stars, and the moon. The rays of the sun are full of power that warms our planet. The moon pulls the tides back and forth in the oceans. Gravity is so powerful it holds the sun, the moons, and all of the planets in place! The power of nature is a force that can change the world slowly or in an instant. Without the power of nature we wouldn't exist and the earth would be dark and cold. We have no control over nature and it is the most powerful force in the world.

Another kind of power you might think of is the power we get from natural resources like oil, petroleum, and gasoline. We use the energy from these natural resources to drive our cars and heat our homes. We generate power in the form of electricity so we can light up our houses, power our computers and our televisions, and cook our food. Without the power we get from natural resources we would have a tough time living our daily lives.

All of the power in the world is nothing without the power of good people. Every day you are surrounded by people who do great things. It is everyday people like you and me that use our power to make a positive impact on the world. Right now, this very minute, there are people all over the world that are taking care of their families, going to work, studying, and helping others in need. The power of people is what makes the world go around.

Of course it is true that there are some people who have a lot of power! They are the leaders in our communities and countries around the world. Leaders make decisions that impact our lives and it takes good leaders to make the right decisions. A good leader is smart and wise and kind. He or she puts other people's needs, wants, and desires first. A good leader listens to people and works together with teams to plan and design programs that will help the world. A powerful leader that is smart and has a good heart can help the world and make positive changes for us to have a better life.

But what happens when a leader uses their power in a negative way? When a leader makes bad decisions people's lives are affected and the world can become a scary place. It is the response of ordinary people like you and me that can help to make positive changes in the world. People joining together to help each other and making their voices heard can make a difference!

So now you know a little bit more about power and you have learned that power can be both good and bad. But there is one kind of power that is the most important power of all and that is the power that is inside each one of you!

You have a good heart and brain that will help you to make smart decisions! You can use the power of your brain to study hard so that you can become a community leader that will make good decisions. You can use the power of your heart to care about others and help people who are in need. You can use the power of your brain and your heart together to stand up for injustice when you see it, whether it is on the playground, in your own community, or in the world!

So look for ways to use your power; it's not as hard as you might think! Some of the most simple acts of kindness are the most powerful. When you smile at someone you are using your power to make them feel good. When you help someone you are using your power to make their life easier. When you speak kindly to someone you are using your power to make them feel happy. The kindness you show to others is more powerful than words.

So use your power in a positive way every day. Be kind, care about others, and take a stand when you see negative power in the world. Power can be used for good and power can be used for evil. But don't ever forget that whatever happens, it is the power within **YOU** that can make a difference.

After Reading

Discussion Questions

1. What examples of power does the author mention in this passage? What are some additional examples of power?
2. What is the difference between positive and negative power? Give examples of each.
3. What characteristics mentioned in the text describe the power of a good leader?
4. How can people use their power to make a positive impact on the world?
5. What does the author mean when she says there is power in acts of kindness such as a smile, a kind word, and lending a helping hand?

Charting Activity

Together with the class determine the main idea of the text and list the key supporting details.

Closing Activity: Write/Pair/Share

Write/Pair/ Share

Distribute Global Concepts Journals to the class and give them an opportunity to start a new chapter for Power. Ask them to write the definition for Power and record the Compelling Question in their journals. ***How can people use their power to make the world a better place?***

Writing Prompt

KG–2: With teacher support write a response and draw a picture to describe how people can use their power to make the world a better place.

3–5: Write a response to the compelling question.

Give students time to write their response and share it with a partner.

Informational Story Map–Power

Name_____ Date_____

What is the Main Idea of the story?	List the details below that support the Main Idea:

What did you learn about POWER from reading the story?

What new ideas do you have to add to the story?

Figure 6.1

LESSON 2

Read Aloud: Narrative Text, "The Peace Club"

Key Standards

- **CCRL.1:** Refer to details and examples in a text when explaining what the text says explicitly and drawing inferences from the text.

Objective

- I can refer to details and give examples to show how each Global Concept is demonstrated in the story.

Focus Skill: Inferencing

Procedure

Before Reading

Ask students if they think they have the power to solve the problems in their classroom. Tell them that today's story is about a group of students that do just that!

During Reading

Tell students to listen to the story and notice how all five Global Concepts are demonstrated.

THE PEACE CLUB

It seemed like another ordinary day at school. The morning bell rang and the kids ran into the building as usual pushing and shoving each other as they made their way through the halls.

In room 202 the morning announcements started as I slipped quietly into my seat and watched our teacher, Mrs. Petty, write our schedule for the day on the board.

8:20 Math
9:20 English Language Arts
10:20 Class Meeting
11:30 Lunch
12:15 Social Studies
1:15 Science
2:15 Music
3:10 Dismissal

"Good Morning, Class," Mrs. Petty said. "Let's get our math books out and get started. We have a busy day ahead of us."

Johnny Bates raised his hand, "Mrs. Petty, why are we having a class meeting today?"

"We have some important issues that we need to talk about so I decided that today we would include it in our schedule." We all wondered what the problem was and it was on our minds as we went through our morning classes.

Mrs. Petty gave us a break and asked us to move our desks so we could sit in a circle together in the middle of the room. Now we were really puzzled and a few kids were rolling their eyes at each other as we began to reorganize the classroom.

We all sat in a circle on the floor, including Mrs. Petty. Some of the kids were pushing, trying to make space, and everyone was trying to sit with their friends. It got noisy and seemed to take forever for kids to get settled and finally Mrs. Petty had to say something. "It doesn't matter who you sit next to, just take a seat!"

The kids scrambled and it got quiet. She started to talk slowly. "It has come to my attention that there are some students in my class that aren't happy and even feel uncomfortable at school. I have been told that there is a lot of mean-spirited teasing among kids on the playground. Some of you are feeling left out and are even afraid to come to school."

I looked around and saw a lot of students with their heads down; no one looked happy, and no one was saying a word. Mrs. Petty was right. It happened in our class and across the school every day. Some kids are made fun of because of the clothes they wear or how they look. There are a few bullies on the playground that pick on kids and start fights. The girls have divided into a few groups and are mean to each other. There were even times when I didn't want to go to school because sometimes kids were mean to me, too. I hated it and I was glad Mrs. Petty was bringing us together, but I just couldn't see how she was going to be able to help.

"When I was a young girl," Mrs. Petty began, "I remember being in a school where there were some mean kids. My mother was a single parent and she had to work long hours every day just so she could pay our rent and put food on the table. My clothes weren't always the most fashionable, but they were always clean. I received free lunch from the cafeteria because we were a low-income family. Of course there were days when I had fun at school and played with my friends. But there were some days that I felt left out. One of those days I will never forget.

"Some girls were gathered on the playground in a circle and whispering to each other. I saw them and started walking over to them to see what was going on. One of them turned around and called out to me, 'Sarah, this doesn't involve you so just go away.'

"I stopped in my track and walked away. The girls acted funny around me for the next couple days. I found out later they were talking about a birthday party that I wasn't invited to. It hurt and it took me a long time to get over it. Eventually a few of the girls in my class came to me and said they were sorry and told me the party was no fun, but the damage had been done."

We looked at each other and felt our heart catch in our throat as we thought about similar situations that had happened in our class.

Mrs. Petty gave each one of us a whiteboard and marker. "Please think about what we can do to make our class better for everyone. How can we do a better job making sure that everyone feels included and becomes friends? Together we have the power to make our class a wonderful place for all students to learn and be the best that they can be. I am not going to ask you to share what you think the problems are—I think you already know. What I want to know are your thoughts and solutions. Please write your ideas on your boards and be ready to share."

Kids looked at each other and a few started to write. A couple of the boys started laughing and Mrs. Petty flashed them her "look" and they started writing. Once everyone had written we were asked to go around in the circle and share. Some of the stuff kids wrote was really dumb; *be nice; bring everyone candy; send the mean kids to the principal; cancel recess.* Mrs. Petty patiently listened to every idea. When it was down to the last few kids to share it didn't look like anyone had a great idea. It was Billy's turn and what he wrote on his board surprised us all. *Peace Club.*

At first no one said a word and we all kind of looked at each other. Finally, I raised my hand, "I like the idea of the Peace Club."

"Me, too," responded Mrs. Petty. "Billy, can you tell us more about your idea."

Billy looked around and he finally spoke up. "I think that if we had a club that promoted Peace in our classroom and even in the school, we would start being nicer to each other."

"What do you think, Class? Do you think a Peace Club would help? If so, what would our Peace Club look like?"

The first one to speak was Marta, "I like the idea and if we had a club we could make a motto, signs, and even pledges that would help us all to be kinder to each other."

"Yeah, and we could have meetings and do activities and make projects to promote Peace in the school," chimed in Dexter.

The class started to get excited and I could tell by Mrs. Petty's face that she liked the idea. "Ok, Class," she said, "let's vote! Go back to your seats and I will give you a slip of paper to write yes or no to the Peace Club." Kids quickly moved the desks back and returned to their seats. We voted and Billy picked up our folded slips of paper. Together with Mrs. Petty he counted and tallied the votes. Quite dramatically, Mrs. Petty opened each ballot: *yes; yes; yes; yes* . . .!" The count went on and it was unanimous that everybody in the class wanted to start a Peace Club.

It was almost lunchtime and Mrs. Petty looked at all of us and smiled. "I am proud of all of you and I am excited about the Peace Club, too.

Think of your ideas for the club at recess and after lunch we will take the whole afternoon to plan our club. Remember, be nice to each other at recess!"

We ate our lunch together and ran outside to play. For the first time our class was actually kind to each other on the playground. We had so much fun and we couldn't wait until we went back to class to plan our Peace Club.

That afternoon we elected a Peace Club President; of course we picked Billy because it was his idea. We wrote our motto: **Be kind to others and create Peace wherever you go**. We wrote our pledge and everyone signed it.

Peace Pledge

I will not judge others based on their appearance, their culture, or their religious beliefs.
I will use my words to solve problems.
I will stand up to injustice and help others in need.
I will take actions needed to make the world a better place.

We had fun working together all afternoon and created banners and signs to hang in our classroom and even in the halls of our school. Mrs. Petty invited our principal to come see our project and he was so excited that he wanted the whole school to join the club!

When we went home that day we felt really good about school. Our class had already come together just working on the project. Over the next few days we hung our signs in the hallways throughout the school. Our class visited other classrooms to tell them about the Peace Club and they all signed the Peace Pledge.

It was such a huge success that the local paper interviewed our class and wrote a big article about our Peace Club. We even got our picture in the paper. The heading of the article was, *"Kids use their Power to create Peace in the world!"*

The Mayor even had a Peace Day celebration in the park and the whole town came together. Families dressed in their best clothes and brought picnics to share their favorite foods. Local leaders spoke to help spread the word of Peace. We played games and danced to music from different countries around the world. Our class was awarded the "Peace Award" and we all went on stage together with Mrs. Petty to accept it. It was the best day ever!

After that day people started to change. No longer were people judged by who they were or where they came from. People were kind and friendly to each other when they met on the streets. Neighbors helped each other and became friends. Soon our town was the friendliest and happiest town in the region.

So this is our story. Mrs. Petty encouraged me to write it down and share it because she said other schools might want to start their own Peace Clubs. Imagine what the world would be like if kids around the world became united and used their power to promote Peace? After all, it just might take kids to show the adults how to do it!

—Kristen

After Reading

Discussion Questions

1. What was the main problem in the story? How did Mrs. Petty help her students to solve the problem?
2. How did the Peace Club help students come together at school? How did the school change?
3. What do you think the author meant when she wrote *Peace is powerful and it starts with each one of us*?
4. How would a Peace Club help your classroom and school?

Charting Activity

Together with the class create a concept map to show how all five Global Concepts are demonstrated in this story.

Global Concepts Wheel

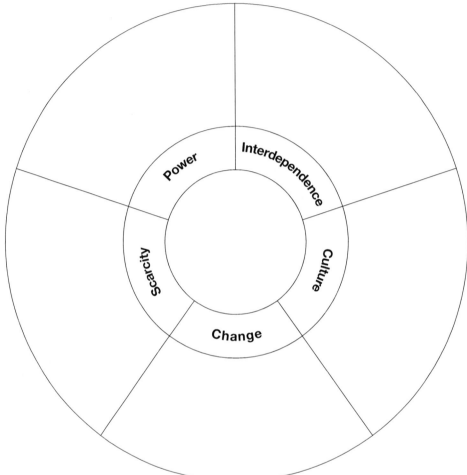

Insert a story title or historical event in the center of the wheel. Describe how each concept is demonstrated in the outer wheel.

Figure 6.2 Circle of Global Concepts

Written Response: Write/Pair/Share

KG–2: With teacher support write a story and draw a picture about your favorite part of the story.

3–5: Do you think a Peace Club would make a difference at schools? Why or why not?

Extension Activity: Your class might really be inspired to start their own Peace Club. Help them create their own club following the ideas the kids had in the story!

What Does Peace Look Like?

Activity 1: Charting ideas about peace

Objective

- I can imagine what peace looks like at home, at school, in my community, and in the world.

Resources

Charting; graphic organizer

Procedure

Creating peace in the classroom is a great start to bringing Peace to the world. But first, students need to have a vision of what Peace will look like at home, at school, in their own community, and in the world. Begin the discussion by asking students what they imagine a peaceful world would look like. *Tell students that once they have an idea of what a peaceful world looks like they can use their power to help make that dream come true!*

Together with the students use this graphic organizer to chart their ideas.

What does Peace look like?

Table 6.1

AT HOME	AT SCHOOL	IN OUR COMMUNITY	IN THE WORLD

Activity 2: My Picture of Peace

Students will create their own picture of what peace looks like using the ideas from the chart they created in Lesson 1. Remind students that each one of us has the power to bring peace to the world. Tell students that they will hang their pictures in the hallway to share their vision of Peace with the school!

Objective

I can create a picture of "Peace" to share my vision with the class.

Procedure

Students can choose one idea from the chart to create their own picture of peace. Ask them to label their picture, "Peace is . . .," with a description of what is happening in the picture. Give students a choice of a variety of paper, markers, colored pencils, crayons, and paint to create their own vision of Peace. Display the pictures in the classroom and throughout the school to help promote peace in the school.

My Global Concepts Mini Book

Students will create their own "Global Concepts Mini Book," to give them an opportunity to review and reflect on what they have learned about each concept.

Objective

I can design my own Global Concepts Mini Book to demonstrate what I learned about the Global Concepts: Change, Interdependence, Culture, Scarcity, and Power.

Procedure

1. Review the concepts, starting with Change, using the Global Concept Cards.
2. Give students their Global Concepts Journals to use as a reference to create their own Global Concepts Mini Book.
3. Students will create their own, Mini Book to show what they learned about each concept. Each mini book will have a colorful cover and at least five pages, one for each concept.
4. Give students time across several days to create their mini books. Encourage students to write about what they learned about each concept and draw pictures that represent each one.
5. Give students an opportunity to share their mini books in small groups and display them in your classroom to showcase your students' learning about Global Concepts.

Additional Lesson Ideas and Resources

Celebrate with your class when they have completed lessons for all five Global Concepts. This is a perfect time for you to invite parents in for a Global Concepts Celebration!

Global Concepts Celebration

Invite parents to a Global Concepts Celebration. This is a great opportunity for parents to see firsthand what their children have learned. Students will have fun planning the celebration, creating invitations and displays, and, of course, preparing their skits to present to their parents. This is also a great time for parents to bring in their favorite foods to share for a multicultural celebration!

Skits

Students work together in small groups to create skits to demonstrate each Global Concept. Assign each group a different concept to write their own skit to teach and demonstrate the meaning of each concept. Give them time to create the skit, make props, and practice acting out their skits. Students can present their skits to other classes or to parents and community members at your Global Concepts Celebration!

Leaders with Power: *Wax Museum*

Share a variety of biographies of famous leaders with your students. Ask students to choose one to read and create a monologue that will tell about the leader's life. What makes this person powerful and how did they use their power to make the world a better place? Give students time in class to practice and encourage them to dress like the person they chose. Invite parents and students to your Wax Museum to listen to your students presentations. Arrange your students in a circle and ask the visitors to the museum to move around the circle and push the button on the student's hand to listen to their monologue. (The whole monologue should fit on one note card!)

Global Concepts Wheel

Now that students have learned all five Global Concepts they can begin to apply them to books and stories they have read and historical and current events they are studying. Using the Global Concepts as a framework will help students to gain new insights and understanding to whatever topics they are studying.

Big Ideas about Power

- Governments are needed to provide protection, guarantee the rights of their citizens, and promote social order.
- Throughout history people and nations have dominated others for the sake of political, economic, and social power.
- Different forms of government have organized society to ensure stability.
- Leaders have power to make decisions that will help make life better for those they serve.
- Problem solving, negotiation, and conflict resolution are important skills necessary for people to coexist in the twenty-first century.
- Everyone has power to help themselves, their families, their community, and the world.

Power Vocabulary

Table 6.2

Leader	Fairness	Law	Rules
Roles	Power and Control	Consequences	Conflict/Resolution
Decision Making	Authority	Government	Issues
Defense	Peace	Cooperation	Human Rights

Applying the Concept of Power across the Curriculum

Math: place value, expanded numerals

Social Studies: forms of government, branches of government, roles of leaders, laws, conflict, history

Science: chemistry, physics, nature, weather

Bibliography for Global Concepts Books: Power

Giraffes Can't Dance (K–2)

Author: Giles Andrede
Illustrator: Guy Parker-Rees

Gerald is the only animal in the jungle that can't dance! He feels bad enough about his lack of rhythm and coordination, but to make it all worse the animals make fun of him! This story illustrates the negative impact of bullying; however, Gerald uses his own Power to come out on top. This story is fun to read and the illustrations are gorgeous! Your students will learn about Power as it is illustrated through the plight of poor Gerald!

Freedom in Congo Square (3–5)

Author: Carole Boston Weatherford
Illustrator: R. Gregory Christie

Carole Boston Weatherford has a gift for bringing the realities of American History and the Black experience to children in a subtle and entertaining way. She uses rhyme to tell the true story of Congo Square in New Orleans. The beautiful illustrations by Mr. Christie enhance the story with vivid and realistic scenes of everyday life on the plantation. The use of power is clearly shown here as the plantation owners use their power to control the slaves, and the slaves use their power to survive. There is real joy in the celebration in Congo Square at the end of the week!

The Librarian of Basra: A True Story from Iraq (3–5)

Author/Illustrator: Jeanette Winter

Alia Muhammad Baker worked for fourteen years as the librarian in Basra, Iraq. The library was a place where people who loved books gathered and shared ideas. When her country suffered from war and destruction Alia used her power to save the priceless collection of books from being destroyed. This true story is based on the events that happened when the invasion of Iraq reached Basra on April 6, 2003. The books are still hidden and Alia is waiting for her dream of a new library to be rebuilt.

Each Kindness (3–5)

Author: Jacqueline Woodson
Illustrator: E.B. Lewis

There have been times in all of our lives when we were not kind to someone that needed a friend. This story illustrates beautifully how being unkind hurts others, but it also hurts ourselves. Chloe turns away from the new girl, Maya, and misses many opportunities to show her kindness. When her teacher does a lesson on kindness in the classroom Chloe realizes what she has done, but it may be too late to make it up to Maya. Being kind to others is a powerful way to make a difference in the world.

The Other Side (2–5)

Author: Jacqueline Woodson
Illustrator: E.B. Lewis

Two little girls, one African American and one white, live next door to each other, separated only by a fence. As the two girls get to know each other they move closer and closer to the fence, even though both their mamas told them not to cross to the other side. They use their Power to get to know each other despite of their mothers' warning and the social norms at the time. As they become friends they sit together on the fence and eventually jump rope. This story illustrates not only the changes in society, but the changes in the girls and their mothers as they cross racial boundaries.

Martin's Big Words: The Life of Dr. Martin Luther King Jr. (K–5)

Author: Doreen Rappaport
Illustrator: Bryan Collins

This book is my favorite Read Aloud book about Dr. Martin Luther King. Not only are the highlights of his life shared in a thoughtful way, but his "Big Words" are illustrated throughout the story. Dr. King was a powerful man that made a positive change in the world for all people, but it is his powerful words that will give us our direction for the future to carry on his legacy.

Malala Yousafzai: Warrior with Words (3–5)

Author: Karen Leggett Abouraya
Illustrator: L.C. Wheatley

This is the second book about Malala that I am recommending for you to read to your class, but this one has an additional important lesson in it! "Our words can change the world!" is one of Malala's famous quotes and it is a message that our students need to hear. Words are powerful and we can help to make a difference in the world by using our words to speak and to write about our dreams for the world. I would use this book to not only demonstrate the power of words, but I would also use it to show students how powerful they are when they use their words to help make a difference in the world.

Bully (3–5)

Author: Patricia Polacco
G.P. Putnam's Sons; a division of Penguin Young Readers Group

Leave it to Patricia Polacco to come out with one of the best books about Bullying I have ever read. It covers it all—a new girl at school tries hard to fit in and finds herself in the middle of a test cheating scandal that is spread on social media across the school. The story is full of opportunities for those important discussions teachers all want to have with their students about bullying and the proper use of social networking. However, it comes right down to Lyla's decision to do the right thing that makes the story such a meaningful and important story to read to your students! This story will hit home to every one of your students as they see how the Global Concept of Power is used in both positive and negative ways.

GOAL! (3–5)

Author: Mina Javaherbin
Illustrator: A.G. Ford

If you are looking for a multicultural book that will appeal especially to boys I recommend this one! Set in South Africa, this is a story about a group of young men who play soccer in the streets. However, one of them has to be on the lookout for bullies! The strength of the boys' friendship and teamwork, plus the role of the bullies, is a wonderful illustration of Power.

Sheikh Zayed (3–5)

Author: Francis LaBonte
Jerboa Books, Dubai, UAE

Sheikh Zayed is well known and revered in the United Arab Emirates. He is the father of their nation and laid the foundation for the strong country that it is today. He was a simple and humble man but he had a vision for his country. I have included this book for you to share with your students an example of a strong Muslim leader to help promote cross-cultural understanding and respect among your students.

Number the Stars (4–5)

Author: Lois Lowry

This story is told through the eyes of ten-year-old Annemarie whose family shelters her best friend, Ellie Rosen, during the dark era in Denmark when Jews were "relocated" by Nazi Germany. Students will learn firsthand the impact of the negative power of the Nazi regime and the positive power of one family that takes a risk to help a young Jewish girl.

Rickshaw Girl (3–5)

Author: Mitali Perkins
Illustrator: Jamie Hogan

This chapter book would be a great read-aloud story for teachers of students in grades 3–5. It's a story that beautifully illustrates all five Global Concepts. It tells about the life of ten-year-old Naima who lives in Bangladesh. Her father earns a meager living as a rickshaw driver and can barely put food on the table. He has been blessed with two daughters but no sons. Naima dresses like a boy to earn money to help her father. What she discovers is that there are other women also starting to work and together, they use their power to slowly change traditions.

7

Implementing Global Concepts in Your School

Will the Global Concepts work at our school?

You may be wondering if the Global Concepts program will be a good "fit" for your school. I understand your concern. However, I want to assure you that the Global Concepts program can become an integral part of your school whether it is public, private, International, or faith based.

To illustrate how Global Concepts works let me share the story of three very different schools that have successfully used the Global Concepts and adapted them to their own school's unique culture, programs, and curriculum.

Lincoln International Studies School, Kalamazoo, Michigan

The Global Concepts were first used in 1998 at Lincoln International Studies School, a Title I Public School, in Kalamazoo, Michigan, where I was the school principal. We developed our Magnet School theme and curriculum based on five Global Concepts from the Michigan Social Studies Standards. Teachers created lessons to introduce each concept. Classrooms had their own International Address and classroom environments reflected the culture of the country that class represented. As concepts were introduced teachers applied them not only to their International Address, but across the curriculum. Teachers identified multicultural books for each concept and used shared reading time during our literacy block to read and discuss the stories that illustrated each Global Concept. The school truly became an International

Studies School as students were immersed in culture as they applied the Global Concepts across the curriculum.

The Alfred and Adele Davis Academy, Atlanta, Georgia

In 2003 I moved to Atlanta, Georgia, and took the position of Lower School Principal at The Alfred and Adele Davis Academy. I introduced the Global Concepts to the Lower School staff and they quickly embraced the concepts and took them a step further as they applied them to their curriculum. The Davis Academy is a highly regarded Reform Jewish Day School and these concepts complemented their Judaic Studies curriculum. Books and stories with Jewish themes that illustrated each Global Concept were chosen for every grade level. The Davis Academy staff systematically introduced the concepts, beginning with "Change" as they started the school year. Each grade level teacher received a kit with the outline for the curriculum and the anchor books for each concept. The Global Concepts fit beautifully with the program at Davis, which had a strong academic program with a focus on Judaism, the study of Israel and the history of the Jewish People. In addition, each grade level adopted community service projects that are still part of the strong tradition of "*Tikkun olam*, Healing the World" at the Davis Academy.

The Maccabi Academy, Asheville, North Carolina

In 2009 I had a unique opportunity to lead another Jewish School in Asheville, North Carolina. The Maccabi Academy was a small but mighty school with the most remarkable staff, parents, and students. At the start of the year I not only trained the staff, but I also informed the school board and parents about the Global Concepts. Maccabi Academy embraced the concepts and quickly added them to their curriculum. The concepts spurred the students to think about needs within their community. They adopted their own Mitzvah project and took an active part in collecting, delivering, and shelving food at a local food bank. Maccabi Academy students saw firsthand how the concepts can be applied as they put Change, Interdependence, Culture, Scarcity, and Power into action.

I shared the stories of these three very different schools to show that any school can adopt the Global Concepts program. Whatever your school's focus and theme, Global Concepts will provide a framework to help your students to become Global Citizens and enrich your curriculum and programs.

Formalizing the Global Concepts Program

The Global Concepts program was well received at each of the three schools and each school used the concepts to enrich its curriculum and theme. However, the program was never formally written down or articulated in a way that other teachers and schools could adopt the program and use it at their schools. Former staff in each of these schools have encouraged me to formalize the program so the Global Concepts could be used by any teacher at any school.

I have taken what I remember and created new stories and lessons based on each concept so a teacher could have an easy-to-use resource to teach their students the Global Concepts. I have also connected the lessons to important Social Studies and English Language Arts standards so teachers can apply the concepts to their own curriculum and lessons.

I have been motivated by my friends, colleagues, and former teachers who have encouraged me to write this book. However, the biggest reason I have written this book is because of what I see happening in the world today. It is my hope that, maybe in some small way, the lessons children learn through the program will help them to be good people that will work hard to make the world a better place. It is my hope that your school will embrace the Global Concepts and bring the world to your students. The rest of this chapter will be suggestions from me based on my experience to help you to introduce the Global Concepts to your staff and your students.

Implementing the Global Concepts Program School-Wide

The Global Concepts will add focus and excitement to your school program and it will also add rigor to your curriculum. Students, parents, and the community will also become more engaged with the school as they work together with you to bring the world to your students.

The decision to use the Global Concepts program is one that needs to be made together. Involving administrators, teachers, and parents in the decision to move forward is paramount to the success of the program. If you are the school leader and are considering adopting the Global Concepts to your school program, I recommend that you introduce the program to the stakeholders in your school. Share with them copies of this book and hopefully they will like what they see and be excited to get started. Also, if you are excited about the program and have good reasons to implement it in your school I am sure you will be able to share that enthusiasm with others.

First Steps

Form a Global Concepts Committee

I have always relied on the resourcefulness and creativity of my staff to implement any program from our school-wide literacy program to the school play. Seek out members of your staff to serve on the Global Concepts committee. Their planning and leadership will not only get the program started in your school but provide ongoing planning and direction throughout the school year.

Make sure you include your media specialist if you are lucky enough to have one! They will provide valuable insight and leadership to the planning and implementation of the Global Concepts program. They also hold the keys to the treasure of resources in the building, which includes a rich collection of books and technology.

Give the committee these tasks to get started.

1. Create a calendar for the introduction of each concept and identify lessons, books, and projects for each grade level.
2. Develop a plan to Globalize the classrooms and the school environment.
3. Plan staff training to introduce the concepts to teachers and give them an opportunity to apply the concepts at an adult level and plan lessons for their students.
4. Plan special events to be held school-wide to celebrate Global Concepts, showcase student work, and provide cultural programs and events.

Use Your Resources

In addition to the Global Concepts Handbook for teachers, you will need a wide variety of supplemental materials to bring this program to life. However, I recommend that you work with your committee to come up with a plan. What resources do you already have in your school?

1. Does each classroom have a current map and globe?
2. What books does your library already have that support each concept?
3. What artifacts from different cultures do you already have in your school?
4. In addition to your own country's flag, do you have on display flags from other countries where your students are from?

5. What resources are available to us through our school family and the community?
6. What multicultural books are already in your library?

Once you have done an inventory of what you have, make sure that teachers and students have access to the resources. The first year teachers implement the program they may find additional multicultural books and artifacts that they want for their classroom. Purchase books connected to the Global Concepts for your library. Ask teachers to create a wish list of books and resources they want to add to their Global Classroom environment and provide funds from your school budget. If your budget is tight, like it is for most schools, access funding through grants. Teachers can apply for grants through *www.gofund.com*. Schools can apply for grants through Federal and private nonprofit programs. Local businesses in your community are also good places to look for funds to support your Global Concepts program.

Create a Global Environment

Look around your school. Does it reflect the diversity of your students and your community? Does it have a Global look? To help your students to think Globally it is important to immerse them into the world at school. Post the Global Concept cards in the office and the hallways to help everyone to be aware of the concepts. Hang flags in the hallways from countries that represent your student body. Decorate the halls with pictures and posters of different sites throughout the world. Display a large map wall mural in your hallways. Give your students and staff an opportunity to put pictures of themselves that have traveled and connect them with string to the location. These are just a few ideas to get you started, but I am sure you have the idea. Whatever you can do to help kids to connect to the world will be a great way to support your Global Concepts program!

Staff Development

Teachers will benefit from professional development to help them to become Global Educators and understand the Global Concepts at an adult level. Teachers will continue to discover ways to apply the concepts across the curriculum as they teach the lessons that are included in the Global Concepts Handbook. The program will continue to build as teachers gain their own understanding of the concepts and begin to recognize the connections that naturally occur throughout the curriculum.

I recommend that you introduce the Global Concepts program with at least one of the activities below to make your staff meetings and training interactive and fun! Training can continue throughout the year as you devote part of your staff meeting time to the Global Concepts program.

Introducing Global Concepts to Staff

Teachers will also have fun learning about the concepts through interactive activities done together with their peers. Here are some fun and simple ways to introduce the concepts and get your staff excited about implementing the Global Concepts program in their classroom.

Group Charting Activity: Adults already have an understanding of the concepts, so try starting your training to find out what they already know and believe about the concepts. Divide your staff into five groups and give them chart paper and a variety of colored markers. Let them express themselves by creating a chart about the concept they have been assigned. Give each group an opportunity to share their chart. Keep these charts on display in the teachers' work room!

Expressing the Global Concepts through the Arts! Teachers don't often get a chance to express themselves artistically. Gather a variety of art materials and put them out on a table for teachers to choose. As teachers come into the training randomly give them each a card with one Global Concept. Assign them the task to create a piece of art that expresses their meaning of the concept. Give them a time limit and ask them to display their masterpiece!

Act It Out: Put teachers into groups to work together to plan a skit to showcase the Global Concept they are assigned. Each skit should demonstrate the Global Concept in a real-life situation. The skits should have a beginning, middle, and end that show a clear problem and solution. Of course, they will perform their skits for the whole group!

Connecting Global Concepts Across the Curriculum: Teachers have a deep understanding of the content and curriculum that they are teaching. However, they may need support at the beginning to see how the Global Concepts link. Form groups of teachers that teach the same grade level or content areas to link content topics to each Global Concept. Ask each group to create a mind map, showing the links as a visual reminder to help them with their planning.

Go Global at Staff Meetings: Think of ways to bring the world to your staff through a variety of short presentations and activities at staff meetings.

Consider inviting local leaders and community members to speak on important topics related to the Global Concepts.

Here are some ideas:

1. Invite a community leader or a university professor to speak to your staff about various topics connected to the Global Concepts to help them to gain more adult understanding from experts in the field.
2. Invite a first-generation refugee or immigrant to share their stories with your staff.
3. Speakers from the Red Cross, Rotary, and other national and international service agencies are eager to share their stories.
4. Invite multicultural storytellers, musicians, and authors to perform and share their stories with your staff.

Take Your Staff into the Community: Look for opportunities to bring the world to your teachers. Instead of a traditional staff meeting consider using that time for field trips and excursions to local international sites. Here are some ideas your staff will enjoy!

1. Visit museums in your community and ask for a special tour of important international exhibits.
2. Visit international markets or restaurants.
3. Attend cultural events and programs as a staff.
4. Visit the local shelters and food banks to see and hear firsthand what they do.
5. Arrange a tour for your staff to the local church, temple, and mosque so they can experience and learn about other faiths and cultures.
6. Give the staff an opportunity to share their travel experiences at a meeting.
7. Adopt a community service project with the staff that will benefit your school, your community, or the world.

Create a Global Village in Your School: The Global Concepts will give your school an opportunity to create a Global Village that reflects the heart of the program. Teaching **Change** will not only help your students to understand and accept change, but you and your staff will also gain new insight to the changes you are facing as educators. The Global Concept of **Interdependence** will bring to life ways that you, your staff, students, parents, and the community are connected and can support one another. As your school explores the Global Concept of **Culture**, you will have fun together, celebrating diversity as you learn about each other and people around the world.

The study of **Scarcity** will provide an opportunity for your students and staff to learn about scarcity issues around the world and develop empathy for others in need. When your school family experiences the Global Concept of **Power,** they will become empowered as they work together to help people in need both at home and around the world.

As your Global Village develops you will see your school family come together as they apply the lessons they are learning through the Global Concepts program. Implementing the program will take planning and effort by you and your staff. It will take the commitment of your teachers to create their Global environments and teach the lessons. But no matter how daunting it may seem, think about what your students will be missing if you don't teach them the Global Concepts.

Teaching your students to understand themselves and the world may be one of the greatest gifts you will ever give them. When students feel like they belong to the Global Village at school they will begin to see their own special place in the world. Global Concepts are not going to solve the world's problems, but they will give our students a better understanding of the world they live in today and hope for the world tomorrow.

Appendix 1
Global Concepts Read Aloud Lesson Planner

Global Concepts Read Aloud Lesson Plan

Story Title_____

Author:_____

Global Concept_____

How is the concept demonstrated?	Common Core/ELA Standard

Vocabulary	Resources: Technology Links:

Questions:

 Before-

During-

After-

Follow Up: Discussion_____ Charting ____ Graphic Organizer ____ Journal Entry

Cross Curriculum Link:

Activity:

Appendix 2

Informational Global Concepts Story Map

Global Concepts Informational Text Map

Title: Author:	Global Concept/Topic
What is the Main Idea or Theme of the text?	**List supporting details:**

What did you learn about _____ from reading the text?

What new ideas can you add?

Appendix 3
Narrative Global Concepts Story Map

Narrative Story Map

Name_____

Title:	Main Character (s)
Author:	

Main Events in the story:	Problem/Solution:

What Global Concept was demonstrated in the story?

What did you learn about the Global Concept _____ from the story?

Appendix 4

Informational Story Map—Change

Informational Story Map–CHANGE

Name_____ Date_____

What is the Main Idea of the story?	List the details below that support the Main Idea:

What did you learn about CHANGE from reading the story?

What new ideas do you have to add to the story?

Appendix 5

Informational Story Map—Interdependence

Informational Story Map–INTERDEPENDENCE	
Name_____ Date _____	
What is the Main Idea of the story?	List the details below that support the Main Idea:

What did you learn about INTERDEPENDENCE from reading the story?

What new ideas do you have to add to the story?

Appendix 6

Informational Story Map—Culture

Informational Story Map–CULTURE

Name_____ Date_____

What is the Main Idea of the story?	List the details below that support the Main Idea:

What did you learn about CULTURE from reading the story?

What new ideas do you have to add to the story?

Appendix 7

Informational Story Map—Scarcity

Informational Story Map–SCARCITY	
Name_____ Date_____	
What is the Main Idea of the story?	**List the details below that support the Main Idea:**

What did you learn about SCARCITY from reading the story?

What new ideas do you have to add to the story?

Appendix 8

Informational Story Map—Power

Informational Story Map–POWER	
Name_____ Date_____	
What is the Main Idea of the story?	List the details below that support the Main Idea:

What did you learn about POWER from reading the story?

What new ideas do you have to add to the story?

Appendix 9

Narrative Story Map—Changes for Charlie

Story Map–*Changes for Charlie*
Name_____ Date_____

Describe Charlie	What is the main problem in the story?

List each Change Charlie went through in the story.	Tell how Charlie Felt about each change.

How did Charlie's feelings change by the end of the story?

What did you learn about, CHANGE, from reading the story?

Appendix 10

Narrative Story Map—A Home for Lucky

Story Map–A Home for Lucky

Name_____ Date_____

Main Characters	Setting of Story

Main Events in the story	Problem/Solution

How was the Global Concept, SCARCITY, demonstrated in the story?

What did you learn about SCARCITY from reading the story?

Appendix 11

Narrative Story Map—Monty and Omar

Monty Goes to School	Omar Goes to Kindergarten

How are they alike?

How are they different?	How are they different?

DRAW A PICTURE OF MONTY

DRAW A PICTURE OF OMAR

Appendix 12

Global Concepts Culture Chart

Global Concepts Culture Chart

People and Region	Food	Shelter	Clothing	Language	Education	Free Time Activities	Holidays and Celebrations

Appendix 13

Story Culture Chart

Story Culture Chart

Title of Story	Main Character/s Description	Setting of story	Food	Clothing	Shelter	School	Way of Life

Appendix 14
Name That Artifact!

Name That Artifact!

Draw a Picture of the Artifact	What is it made of?	How do you think it was made?	What do you think it was used for?	Where in the world is it from?	What more ideas do you have about this artifact?
					Artifact Name?

Appendix 15

Applying the Global Concepts

Applying the Global Concepts

Title_____ Author_____

Think about the story and tell how each Global Concept is Demonstrated.

Change	
Interdependence	
Culture	
Scarcity	
Power	

Appendix 16

Global Concepts Wheel

Global Concepts Wheel

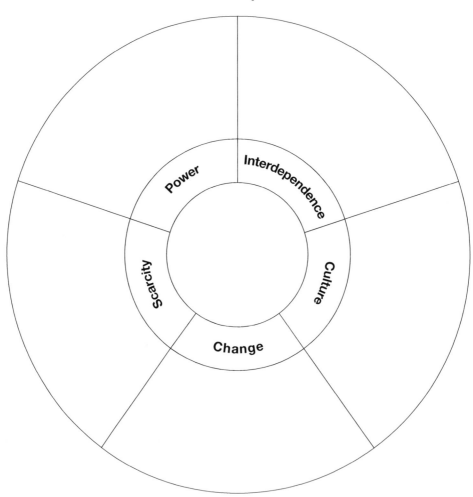

Insert a story title or historical event in the center of the wheel. Describe how each concept is demonstrated in the outer wheel.

Appendix 17

Technology Links to Bring the World to your Students!

www.globalgoals.org
Collaborate with the UN to achieve 17 Global Goals. Videos and lessons available for classroom teachers.

www.mysteryskype.com
Take your class on virtual fieldtrips, partner with classrooms around the world for Skype lessons, Skype Collaboration, Mystery Skype, and Guest Speakers.

www.globalschoolnet.com
Link your students with students from around the world through joining community projects.

www.epals.com
Teachers and students connect with classrooms around the world.

www.culturequest.us
Explore other peoples and cultures through inquiry based classroom projects.

www.teachertube.com
A safe place for teachers to find and post videos to support global Concept lessons.

Apps
Toontastic-3D (FREE)
Students can draw, animate and narrate their own cartoons to broadcast news reports and share their Global Concepts Projects.

YouTube Kids (FREE)
A great app for teachers to locate videos on a wide variety of topics related to the world that connect nicely to each global concept. *Recommended for young children.*

Taylor & Francis eBooks

Helping you to choose the right eBooks for your Library

Add Routledge titles to your library's digital collection today. Taylor and Francis ebooks contains over 50,000 titles in the Humanities, Social Sciences, Behavioural Sciences, Built Environment and Law.

Choose from a range of subject packages or create your own!

Benefits for you

>> Free MARC records
>> COUNTER-compliant usage statistics
>> Flexible purchase and pricing options
>> All titles DRM-free.

Benefits for your user

>> Off-site, anytime access via Athens or referring URL
>> Print or copy pages or chapters
>> Full content search
>> Bookmark, highlight and annotate text
>> Access to thousands of pages of quality research at the click of a button.

REQUEST YOUR **FREE** INSTITUTIONAL TRIAL TODAY

Free Trials Available
We offer free trials to qualifying academic, corporate and government customers.

eCollections – Choose from over 30 subject eCollections, including:

Archaeology	Language Learning
Architecture	Law
Asian Studies	Literature
Business & Management	Media & Communication
Classical Studies	Middle East Studies
Construction	Music
Creative & Media Arts	Philosophy
Criminology & Criminal Justice	Planning
Economics	Politics
Education	Psychology & Mental Health
Energy	Religion
Engineering	Security
English Language & Linguistics	Social Work
Environment & Sustainability	Sociology
Geography	Sport
Health Studies	Theatre & Performance
History	Tourism, Hospitality & Events

For more information, pricing enquiries or to order a free trial, please contact your local sales team:
www.tandfebooks.com/page/sales

 Routledge
Taylor & Francis Group

The home of
Routledge books

www.tandfebooks.com